REGENTS RENAISSANCE DRAMA SERIES

General Editor: Cyrus Hoy
Advisory Editor: G. E. Bentley

A JOVIAL CREW

D0666929

RICHARD BROME

A Jovial Crew

Edited by

ANN HAAKER

UNIVERSITY OF NEBRASKA PRESS · LINCOLN

Regents Renaissance Drama Series

The purpose of the Regents Renaissance Drama Series is to provide soundly edited texts, in modern spelling, of the more significant plays of the Elizabethan, Jacobean, and Caroline theater. Each text in the series is based on a fresh collation of all sixteenth- and seventeenth-century editions. The textual notes, which appear above the line at the bottom of each page, record all substantive departures from the edition used as the copy-text. Variant substantive readings among sixteenth- and seventeenth-century editions are listed there as well. In cases where two or more of the old editions present widely divergent readings, a list of substantive variants in editions through the seventeenth century is given in an appendix. Editions after 1700 are referred to in the textual notes only when an emendation originating in some one of them is received into the text. Variants of accidentals (spelling, punctuation, capitalization) are not recorded in the notes. Contracted forms of characters' names are silently expanded in speech prefixes and stage directions, and, in the case of speech prefixes, are regularized. Additions to the stage directions of the copy-text are enclosed in brackets. Stage directions such as "within" or "aside" are enclosed in parentheses when they occur in the copy-text.

Spelling has been modernized along consciously conservative lines. "Murther" has become "murder," and "burthen," "burden," but within the limits of a modernized text, and with the following exceptions, the linguistic quality of the original has been carefully preserved. The variety of contracted forms ('em, 'am, 'm, 'um, 'hem) used in the drama of the period for the pronoun them are here regularly given as 'em, and the alternation between a'th' and o'th' (for on or of the) is regularly reproduced as o'th'. The copy-text distinction between preterite endings in -d and -ed is preserved except where the elision of e occurs in the penultimate syllable; in such cases, the final syllable is contracted. Thus, where the old editions read "threat'ned," those of the present series read "threaten'd." Where, in the old editions, a contracted preterite in -y'd would yield -i'd in modern spelling (as in "try'd," "cry'd," "deny'd"), the word is here given in its full form (e.g., "tried," "cried," "denied").

Punctuation has been brought into accord with modern practices. The effort here has been to achieve a balance between the generally light pointing of the old editions, and a system of punctuation which, without overloading the text with exclamation marks, semicolons, and dashes, will make the often loosely flowing verse (and prose) of the original syntactically intelligible to the modern reader. Dashes are regularly used only to indicate interrupted speeches, or shifts of address within a single speech.

Explanatory notes, chiefly concerned with glossing obsolete words and phrases, are printed below the textual notes at the bottom of each page. References to stage directions in the notes follow the admirable system of the Revels editions, whereby stage directions are keyed, decimally, to the line of the text before or after which they occur. Thus, a note on 0.2 has reference to the second line of the stage direction at the beginning of the scene in question. A note on 115.1 has reference to the first line of the stage direction following line 115 of the text of the relevant scene.

CYRUS HOY

University of Rochester

Contents

List of Abbreviations

Belman	Thomas Dekker. *The Belman of London* (fourth impression). London, 1616.
Bentley	Gerald Eades Bentley. *The Jacobean and Caroline Stage.* Oxford, 1941–1956.
Brome	Richard Brome. *A Jovial Crew.* Printed for C. Brome. London, 1708.
Camden	William Camden. *Britain.* London, 1610.
Collier	J. P. Collier, ed. *A Select Collection of Old Plays.* Vol. X. London, 1826.
Cotgrave	Randle Cotgrave. *A Dictionary of the French and English Tongues.* London, 1611.
Coxeter	T. Coxeter, ed. *A Select Collection of Old Plays.* Vol. VI. London, 1744.
DNB	*Dictionary of National Biography*
Eng. Vil.	Thomas Dekker. *English Villanies.* London, 1638.
Greg	W. W. Greg. *A Bibliography of the English Printed Drama to the Restoration.* 4 vols. Oxford, 1939–1959.
Harman	Thomas Harman. *A Caveat or Warening for Commen Cursetors.* London, 1573.
Lanthorne	Thomas Dekker. *Lanthorne and Candle-light.* London, 1609.
OED	*Oxford English Dictionary*
Onions	C. T. Onions. *A Shakespeare Glossary.* Oxford, 1911.
Partridge	Eric Partridge. *Shakespeare's Bawdy.* London, 1955.
Phillips	Edward Phillips. *The Mysteries of Love and Eloquence.* London, 1658.
Q1	First Quarto of 1652
Q2	Second Quarto of 1661
Q3	Third Quarto of 1684
Reed	Isaac Reed, ed. *A Select Collection of Old Plays.* Vol. III. London, 1780.

S.D.   stage direction

Sh. Eng. *Shakespeare's England.* 2 vols. Oxford, 1916.

S.P.   speech prefix

Sugden   Edward H. Sugden. *A Topographical Dictionary to the Works of Shakespeare and His Fellow Dramatists.* London, 1925.

Tilley   Morris Palmer Tilley. *A Dictionary of the Proverbs in England in the Sixteenth and Seventeenth Centuries.* Ann Arbor, 1950.

Wright   Joseph Wright. *The English Dialect Dictionary.* Oxford, 1923.

Introduction

DATE AND STAGE HISTORY

The title page of the first edition states that *A Jovial Crew* was presented "at the Cock-pit in Drury-Lane in the year 1641." Since Brome sponsored the publication, there is no reason to doubt the information. According to a 1640 Requests Proceedings Document [1] Brome had left Salisbury Court theater sometime in April, 1639, and by May of that year was writing exclusively for his friend, William Beeston, then managing the King and Queen's Young Company (Beeston Boys) at the Cockpit theater. An allusion to *The Academy of Complements, Philomusus* [2] (entered in the Stationers' Register late 1638 and printed by Humphrey Mosley in 1640) may point to 1640 as an early limit of composition. Concerning the date of performance, Professor Bentley writes: "There are suggestions that the play was planned to open 25 April 1641, or thereabouts." Of the passage at I.i.113–114, wherein Springlove presents his accounts to Oldrents ahead of the reckoning date (" 'Tis yet but thirty days, when I give forty/ After the half-year day, our Lady last"), Bentley notes: "That is, the accounting year began as usual on Michaelmas Day, and the half-yearly accounts were closed on Lady Day (25 March). Springlove was allowed forty days of grace to make up his accounts, or until about 5 May, but here he is after only thirty days, or about 25 April. This same date is suggested later in the scene when Oldrents says, ' 'Tis well-nigh May'." [3]

The probable meaning of Brome's comment in his dedication to Lord Stanley, that his play "had the luck to tumble last of all in the epidemical ruin of the scene" (ll. 26–27), Professor Bentley suggests

[1] Bill of Complaint filed by Salisbury Court Company against Richard Brome, the original document in the London Public Record Office, catalogued as Reg. 2/622 and 723. A complete transcription of the Bill of Complaint and Brome's Answer will be included in my forthcoming article "The Plague, The Theater, and the Poet" in *Renaissance Drama*, ed. S. Schoenbaum.

[2] *A Jovial Crew*, II.i.61–62.

[3] G. E. Bentley, *The Jacobean and Caroline Stage*, Vol. III (Oxford, 1956), 72.

to be that *A Jovial Crew* "was performed on the last day the company acted before they were suppressed by Parliament's order, 2 September 1642."[4] Though there are no contemporary references to the popularity of the play, its many revivals in both the Restoration and eighteenth century, its adaptation into comic opera and its many imitations in the eighteenth century attest its success. Its revival on January 21, 1661, at the new Gibbon's Tennis Court in Vere Street[5] prompted Pepys to see it three times that year (July 25, August 27, and November 1) and again on January 11, 1669, at Drury Lane.[6] Four more performances at Drury Lane are recorded for the seventeenth century, and on November 15, 1689, the play was acted at White Hall before King William and Queen Mary. Its popularity continued well into the eighteenth century. Revived with slight alterations at Drury Lane theater in 1702, it was acted every year at the same theater from 1704 through 1724. The same cast also acted at the new Queen's Theater in 1708 and 1710.

That the lyric charm and the freshness of the songs contributed to the success of *A Jovial Crew* is generally agreed. In 1731 Edward Roome, Sir William Yonge, and Mathew Concanen altered the play into a comic opera which opened February 8 at Drury Lane. In 1760 Covent Garden theater revived the play in its comic opera version, with music arranged by William Bates. It met with amazing success and held the stage, performed several times yearly, for another fifteen years. To offset competition, Drury Lane theater presented *The Ladies Frolic*, altered from Brome's *A Jovial Crew* by James Love [Dance] in 1770, which ran several performances until 1775. The comic opera version was first printed in 1731 with music prefixed to each song, and reprinted in 1732, 1760, 1761, 1766, 1767, 1774, 1780 and 1781.

SOURCE

For the beggar cant and manners Brome certainly used Thomas Harman's *A Caveat or Warning for Common Cursitors* (1573) and Thomas

---

[4] *Ibid.*, p. 71.

[5] For dates of revivals in the seventeenth and eighteenth centuries, see *The London Stage 1660–1800*, ed. William van Lennep, Emmett L. Avery, and A. W. Stone (Carbondale, Illinois, 1965); *History of the Drama and Stage in England 1660–1830*, ed. John Genest (London, 1832); *Drury Lane Calendar*, ed. Dougald MacMillan (Oxford, 1938).

[6] *The Diary of Samuel Pepys*, ed. Henry B. Wheatley (London, 1902).

Dekker's *English Villainies* (1638) and *The Bellman of London* (1608). It is generally agreed that Brome was indebted to Middleton and Rowley's *The Spanish Gipsy*.[7] Its general construction is similar to that of *A Jovial Crew*: each play has two loosely connected plots,[8] a child-recovered theme about which the main action evolves, and a play-within-a-play device used to solve the difficulties in the main action. Such minor particulars in plot as the death of a mother in childbirth, and the beginning and interruption occurring in each play-within-a-play are also similar. Brome may have been influenced in part by Jonson's masque, *The Gipsies Metamorphosed*.[9] Professor Bentley attests the easy accessibility of both sources: "the masque was printed in folio and in duodecimo in 1640; *The Spanish Gipsy* belonged to Beeston's Boys, the company for which Brome was writing, in 1639 . . . and he presumably could use the manuscript in the archives at the Cockpit theatre."[10] Both Dr. Faust and Dr. Floyd have noted the similarities in the beggar commonwealth represented in *A Jovial Crew* and *Beggars' Bush* and have sought to argue Brome's further indebtedness to Fletcher's play, but Professor Bentley sees little evidence of such.

THE PLAY

A Jovial Crew, one of Brome's most rollicking plays, emerged from "sad and tragic days" in which mirth, according to the Prologue, was "a new/ And forc'd thing." "All the arguments I can use to induce you to take notice of this thing of nothing," wrote Brome in the Dedication of the play to Lord Stanley, "is that it had the luck to tumble last of all in the epidemical ruin of the scene." Why does Brome speak of his times as sad, tragic, and epidemical? The national

[7] See E. K. R. Faust, "Richard Brome," in *Archiv fur das Studium der neuren Sprachen*, LXXXII (1889), 53–58; Giles Floyd, "A Critical Edition of Brome's *A Jovial Crew*" (Ph.D Thesis, University of Iowa, 1943), pp. xlvii–lxvi; Bentley, III, 73.

[8] In *A Jovial Crew* are the story of Springlove and his beggar-world and the subplot of Amie and Martin; in *The Spanish Gipsy* are the story of Constanza and her gipsy-world as well as that of Roderigo and Clara.

[9] Faust (p. 56) compares the similarity of Jonson's reference in the masque to a Justice Jug's daughter who ran away with a kinsman of their gipsy captain "and her father pursuing her to the marshes," with the Amie-Martin incident in *A Jovial Crew*.

[10] Bentley, III, 73.

scene before the general closure of the theaters in 1642 was burdened with foreign wars, religious strife, despotic courts, heavy taxation, and increasing threat of civil war. For the creative the times were "anti-ingenious":[11] "instructive recreations"[12] dealing with the ethical and moral concerns of Elizabethan writers such as Shakespeare, Fletcher, and Jonson were outmoded; audiences preferred escapism in the form of spectacle and lavish productions. Worse, a new disease had infiltrated the country, incurable because, according to one of the current prose tracts, "their whole colledge [Physicians] knowes not how to cure this Epidemicall Disease (that like the sweating Sicknesse in times past) raigneth over the whole land, that is, want of money."[13] L. C. Knights best sums up the situation: "Man can adjust himself to the fact of death; he cannot adjust himself to a life disorganized and thwarted, and the root cause of melancholy and discontent is to be found in the social and economic conditions of the time."[14]

It is against this background of economic confusion that Brome sets his play. Money was the great desideratum; and avarice, a common trait. The economic scene teemed with projectors, monopolists, usurers, quacks, and every other representative of economic parasitism. The bourgeoisie vainly attempted to retain, if not augment, luxuries and freedoms to which they already were beginning to be accustomed. Puritan and Cavalier excesses continued to mount. Nothing was stable; country, city, and court were affected. Country gentlemen in fear of losing their estates were "every where readier to sell then to purchase . . . some . . . scarce able to buy them horses to come to petition for their grievances."[15] The anonymous author of *The Distractions of our Times* continues with an account of the effects of internal strife and the rise in pauperism: "Shee [London] hath now little returne of trade, her excellent Artisans cannot get imployment, or finde where to shew their skill, her Mechanicks walke worklesse up and down, or going into the Countrey to visit their friends, some of them can hardly ever finde the way back againe." Nor was there any recourse to religion: "The Citie and Citizens know not well what to doe or trust to, as first, what Religion to professe,

[11] Dedication to Lord Stanley in *A Jovial Crew*, l. 1.
[12] John Hall, commendatory verses to *A Jovial Crew*, l. 1.
[13] *The Distractions of our Times* (edn. 1643), sig. A3.
[14] *Drama and Society in the Age of Jonson* (London, 1937), p. 323.
[15] *Distractions*, sig. A3ᵛ.

itselfe being as it were the conduit head of Sects and Opinions."
Disillusion and pessimism followed. Hence on the eve of the civil war
melancholy had replaced jovial mirth "now grown out of fashion."
Theater audiences demanded escapism from the sordid realities.

Brome, ever sensitive to audience rapport, recognized the symp-
toms, but he also perceived a greater need for homespun mirth and
common sense. Using the same comedic formula applied in *The
Antipodes*, Brome, the "age's doctor" [16] first supplies escape in the
form of time-mellowed memories of the good old days; then, adding
mirth, mixes reality with memories; and finally, within the framework
of the most conventional comedic devices, this time an *Agnus Dei*
leading to the discovery of a long-lost son, allows reality and mirth to
displace escapism and pessimism. The playmaker, who "Never spilt
Ink, except in Comedies," [17] mixes the old with the new, discord with
harmony, realism with idealism, and escapism with the world's
hard realities from which escapism is sought. The play becomes a
study in contrasts and subtle shades of frivolity contesting responsi-
bility. Eventually what were only dreams of happiness become
realities to those who have learned to enjoy happiness by obeying
their Fate. For escape Brome gives his audience a romance "Of
fortune-tellers, damsels, and their squires,/ Expos'd to strange
adventures through the briers/ Of love and fate." [18] Instead of far-
away places, however, he chooses the English countryside, replete
with forests, sparkling streams, open fields, and caroling birds.
Instead of palaces of foreign princes and their court intrigues, he
chooses a representative of the benevolent aristocracy, Squire
Oldrents, who is as generous and revered as he is affluent. In place of
instability Brome substitutes a well-managed three-hundred-year-old
household of contented servants, generously provided for since they
were first picked up as urchins, until now, all graybeards, they take
pride in both their master and their work.

But even this ideal situation is blighted by melancholy which
breeds inevitable discontent. In spite of the efforts of his merry
companion, Hearty, ever ready with his songs, tricks, anecdotes,
dances, and Oldrents' sack, the Squire is sad. He fears the future. A
fortune-teller has told him his children would become beggars. The

---

16 Alexander Brome, commendatory verses to *A Jovial Crew*, l. 33.
17 Richard Brome, commendatory poem, *Lachrymae Musarum* (edn. 1649–
1650), p. 74.
18 *A Jovial Crew*, Prologue, ll. 17–19.

young people can no longer endure the pervading sadness occasioned by the Squire's fear for the future. Hearing the call of spring, Spring-love, the generous young steward, is torn by the conflict of gratitude and concern for Oldrents on one hand, and the desire for freedom from responsibilities and freedom of self-expression on the other. The mirth and revelry among the beggar rout lodging in Oldrents' barn sway his decision, and at the end of Act I he is accepted with open arms as king of the beggars. He leaves the household reflecting: "They dream of happiness that live in state,/ But they enjoy it that obey their fate." Furthermore, the laughter from the beggar-barn wins more converts. Oldrents' daughters and their childhood sweet-hearts are happy to exchange the monotony, the close confinement, and the affectation of conventional behavior for freedom and adventure. Oldrents, too, is attracted by the revelry heard in his barn, but too late does he resolve to purge his house of melancholy. At the end of Act II he has unwittingly driven away the gaiety of youth and love which find no place in his comfortable but melancholy household. In spite of such loss, however, Oldrents decides to forget cares by assuming "jovial mirth,/ Which I will force out of my spleen so freely,/ That grief shall lose her name where I have being" (II.ii.105–107). He increases and extends his generosity to his remaining graybeards, but is yet sick at heart. Beneath the laughter of the beggar rout, he had heard the cry of childbirth and pain which has reminded him of a past deed, and he knows that he but feigns mirth under the incubus of a contrite heart. He can only envy the beggars' full happiness. As yet Oldrents is not heartily merry.

Since the times conspired to make beggars of all, Brome in Act III appropriately presents his audience and cast an escape into a roman-ticized beggar-kingdom, which he sets up as a contrast to Oldrents' affluent household. Whereas Oldrents has the money, the beggars have the mirth and the ability to enjoy what nature provides. Here one finds neither rancor, greed, nor threats. Moreover, each man is his own master. Unfortunates, who found neither money nor mercy in the outside world, seek refuge in the beggar world. The decayed poet finds begging more profitable; the disbarred attorney and turn-coat soldier can use their cunning more honorably in the beggar world; the courtier chooses to beg for pleasure rather than for covetousness. So in this ideal beggar-commonwealth each unfor-tunate and escapee seeks to restore his dignity and to project his "potentia into action."[19] And to those yet on the outside, the beggar-kingdom represents a dream euphoria, a freedom from all restraint. Even Oldrents in his forced gaiety reflects:

> What is an estate
> Of wealth and power, balanc'd with their freedom,
> But a mere load of outward compliment,
> When they enjoy the fruits of rich content?
> Our dross but weighs us down into despair,
> While their sublimed spirits dance i'th' air.
>
> (II.ii.185–190)

Though the desire for mirth and escapism predominate, yet lurking in the background is the world from which all sought escape. Hearty's speeches at the beginning of the play remind us of hoarding usurers, thieving lawyers, quacks in both religion and medicine, fools pricked for sheriffs, suburb justices thriving on fees wracked from underworld practitioners, merciless landlords, courtier-beggars, debtors, inhumane laws, and blind justice. The whole theme of escapism in the beggar-Utopia again reminds the audience of the time's dilemma. From Act III to the end of the play, however, realism gradually supersedes the dream world, until at the end of the play realism and jovial mirth blend. Just as all are not born for weighty offices, neither have all been conditioned for coarse fare. One night's lodging beggar-fashion convinces the youthful beggars-errant that reality is not as sublime as the vision: "We look'd upon them in their jollity, and cast no further" (III.i.28). Springlove consoles them: "this is your birthnight into a new world. And we all know (or have been told) that all come crying into the world, when the whole world of pleasures is before us. The world itself had ne'er been glorious, had it not first been a confused chaos" (III.i.34–38). Besides the discomforts, the converts soon learn that the conventional set speech for courtship has merely been replaced by another set speech for begging, that neither nature nor Springlove will be willing to provide bread gratis, and that often for their pains they must expect only blows and insults in return. Furthermore, under no circumstances dare they show offense. Since, however, they are begging by choice rather than by necessity, they decide to continue this life and make

19 *Existence*, ed. Rollo May, Ernest Angel, Henri F. Ellenberger (New York, 1958), p. 41.

good sport of it. During the course of the act escapees from other households join the beggar world. Amie seeks escape from an enforced marriage with a fool, while her partner ventures opportunism via his master's ward. Young Oliver, a country gentleman of small means, attempts beggar-wenching, thereby escaping the punishment of bastardy, high cost, and the pox in London. In spite of nettling realities, however, Act III ends on a note of revelry, but this time Brome reverses his usual practice of citizens aping the upper class for gentry aping beggars. But aping someone else's role is a ludicrous substitute for heartily playing one's own.

Act IV, scene i, anticipates a senior citizen's dream for the indigent under Oldrents' now merry regime. Increased wages, Christmas bonuses together with rewards of kind gentlemen who have found courteous entertainment during the master's absence (and Oldrents is gone most of the time) have afforded Oldrents' servants sufficient sums to bestow a bit of charity themselves among their kindred. With the dignity of the master himself, they entertain all, using, of course, their master's provisions: " 'tis as fortunate a house for servants as ever was built upon fairy-ground" (IV.i.168–169). What is significant, however, is that the scene ends with the merry Oldrents and Hearty condescending, at last, to leave this small contrived Utopia in order to involve themselves in the less pleasant "business" of the outer world.

The second scene, the rowdiest and merriest of all, brings the audience closer to the chaotic realities of their own world. The parson Under-hedge's wedding ceremony parodies the life-and-mirth-denial doctrine of excessive Puritanism. The virtues of the beggar-commonwealth, listed by the lovers in pretended zeal, reflect again the negative life to which they are soon to return:

> With them there is no grievance or perplexity;
> No fear of war, or state disturbances.
> No alteration in a commonwealth,
> Or innovation, shakes a thought of theirs. . . .
> We have no fear of lessening our estates;
> Nor any grudge with us (without taxation)
> To lend or give, upon command, the whole
> Strength of our wealth for public benefit;
> While some, that are held rich in their abundance,
> (Which is their misery, indeed) will see

Rather a general ruin upon all,
Than give a scruple to prevent the fall.

(IV.ii.90–93, 95–102)

Finally, a masque to be acted extemporaneously along the theme of the ideal commonwealth embraces the follies of the entire nation. Utopia, with her branches and constituencies (the country, city, and court vying for superiority; law and divinity stretching wide throats to appease and reconcile; the army threatening to cudgel them all) is a painful reminder of the national situation. Prophetically enough, the play is interrupted by authorities and the participants arrested.

In Act V, Justice Clack's residence symbolizes the final return to the miserliness, selfishness, and injustice of the very world from which the audience first sought escape. The whole "innumerable army disbanded without pay"—ladies, cavaliers, soldiers, lawyer, fiddlers, poet, players, priest—are reassembled in this world. But the merriment of Hearty and Oldrents, in spite of the wretched hospitality extended to them, infects even Justice Clack, who exclaims, "The virtue of your company turns all to mirth and melody," and he promises that "Law and justice shall sleep, and mirth and good fellowship ride a circuit here tonight" (V.i.219–220, 241–243). The young people are permitted to present their play, plain and to the point, devised to cure Oldrents' melancholy. Past events are re-enacted until Oldrents sees his folly. But not only Oldrents is made to realize his folly; each admits that even a world of escape, once experienced in reality, has drawbacks. It is neither money nor the lack of it that causes the "epidemical ruin of the scene." Brome, the realist, is aware that money keeps the bread baskets, the beef kettles, the beer bumbards filled; keeps graybeards happy; makes possible Springlove's marriage with Amie; keeps Hearty hearty; and even supplies enough sack to quell Tallboy's tears. In fact, money may still be in part the desideratum. But with or without money, it is the true comedic spirit that is needed in the awareness of and the involvement in one's fate. It is Brome's awareness of the needs of his time that prompted Alexander Brome to write in his commendatory verses: "Thou'rt th'age's doctor now, for since all go/ To make us poor, thou mak'st us merry too." Brome shows how the elixir, exalted mirth mixed with generosity, enables all, in whatever station of life, to enjoy their fate. Oldrents, the whole crew, no longer displaced nor seeking escape, are now heartily merry. One of Brome's characters,

Matchil in *The New Academy*, explains further the theory of exalted mirth:

> But come, to end this tedious Scene, in which
> I ha' past the purgatorie of my Passions
> Of Sorrow, anger, feare, and hope at last.
> I am refin'd, sublim'd, exalted, fix't
> In my true Sphere of mirth: where love's my object . . . .
>
> (I.i)

It is a message entirely in accord with the time, then and now. When one considers, among young and old alike, the quest of each to find his proper environment and way of sharing life in order to project his potential into action, one is reminded of Rollo May's words describing "Being-in-the-World": "*World is the structure of meaningful relationships in which a person exists and in the design of which he participates.* Thus world includes the past events which condition my existence and all the vast variety of deterministic influences which operate upon me. But it is these *as I relate to them*, am aware of them, carry them with me, molding, inevitably forming, building them in every minute of relating. For to be aware of one's world means at the same time to be designing it." [20] Add to this the qualities of mirth and generosity, and you have Brome's message, which is particularly evident in this "issue of my old age" (Dedication, l. 3) performed shortly before all plays were to be outlawed during the Puritan regime. Brome was fully aware of his world. Indeed, within the compass of sixteen extant plays, he affords perhaps one of the truest records of the economic, social, and moral climate of a people living in a period of transition. Born sometime during the last years of Queen Elizabeth's reign; apprenticed a play-maker during King James's reign; acknowledged a writer who knows "Beyond his books, men and their actions, too" [21] during King Charles's reign; mentioned deceased in 1653, the first year Oliver Cromwell became Lord Protector—Brome included in the observations of his everyday life both the wistful clinging to an old order considered passé, and the insecurity and unrest of a people still searching for an order yet to be established. And though "Poor he came into th' world, and poor went out," [22]

[20] *Ibid.*, pp. 59–60.
[21] James Shirley, commendatory verses to *A Jovial Crew*, l. 12.
[22] Alexander Brome, commendatory verses in *Five New Playes* (edn. 1659).

reading Brome's plays in conjunction with his time reveals a wealth of seventeenth-century living.

THE TEXT

A Jovial Crew was the last of Brome's plays to be printed during his lifetime. The author's signed dedication to Thomas Stanley and the commendatory verses addressed to Brome, as printed in the first quarto, attest the author's sponsorship of the publication. It is reasonably certain that the manuscript behind the 1652 quarto was prepared for publication by the author. Alexander Brome, in his commendatory verses, writes: "May this so please t'encourage thee, that more/ May be made public, which thou keep'st in store" (ll. 37–38). That Brome had many of his plays in his possession is again suggested in the address to the reader prefixed to the posthumous *Five New Playes* (edn. 1659, sig. A5ᵛ): "As for the Stationers, they bring these Poems as they had them from the Author." Moreover, the many descriptive stage directions which seem designed to accommodate the reader rather than the theater, the ample and correctly indicated entrances and exits, and the consistent designation of characters in both stage directions and speech assignments suggest a fair copy intended for publication. There are no unresolved confusions in the text.

Three editions of *A Jovial Crew* appeared in the seventeenth century: the first edition, in 1652 (Q1); the second edition (printed from Q1) in 1661 (Q2); and the third edition (printed from Q2) in 1684 (Q3). The present text is based on a collation of eight copies of Q1; one each in the Harvard University Library, Yale University Library, Library of Congress, Henry E. Huntington Library; and two each in the Bodleian Library and the British Museum. The only press variant noted was a minor one: the mis-signed sig. L5 in one of the Bodleian quartos was corrected to L3 in all other copies.

ANN HAAKER

California State College at Fullerton

A JOVIAL CREW

To The Right Noble, Ingenious, and Judicious Gentleman, Thomas Stanley, Esq.

SIR,

I have long since studied in these anti-ingenious times to find out a man that might at once be both a judge and patron to this issue of my old age, which needs both. And my blessed stars have flung me upon you, in whom both those attributes concenter and flourish; nor can I yet find a   5
reason why I should present it to you (it being below your acceptance or censure) but only my own confidence, which had not grown to this forwardness had it not been encouraged by your goodness. Yet we all know beggars use to flock to great men's gates. And, though my fortune has cast   10
me in that mold, I am poor and proud, and preserve the humor of him who could not beg for anything but great boons, such as are your kind acceptance and protection. I dare not say (as my brethren use) that I present this as a testimonial of my gratitude or recompense for your favors,   15
for (I protest) I conceive it so far from quitting old engagements that it creates new. So that all that this play can do is but to make more work, and involves me in debts beyond a possibility of satisfaction. Sir, it were a folly in me to tell you of your worth. The world knows it enough and are bold   20
to say fortune and nature scarce ever clubb'd so well. You know, sir, I am old and cannot cringe nor court with the

5. those] *Q 1–2;* these *Q 3.*   22. nor] *Q 1–2;* and *Q 3.*
11. in that] *Q 1–2;* into that *Q 3.*

0.2. *Thomas Stanley*] (1625–1678), only son to Sir Thomas Stanley; author, philosopher, classical scholar, graduated M.A. from Cambridge in 1641. Prominent in literary circles, he was a Maecenas to many less fortunate men of letters, among whom were such associates of Brome's as John Hall and James Shirley. He was a friend of Alexander Brome, who published many of Brome's plays posthumously.

10–11. *cast . . . mold*] i.e., made me a beggar.

12–13. *humor . . . boons*] Apparently this refers to Martial: "Thou begg'st small gifts of great ones, which they yet Deny. To be lesse sham'd, begge gifts more great" ("*Parvarogas magnos*—Epig. 69" in Thomas May's *Selected Epigrams of Martial*, edn. 1629, sig. G5ᵛ).

21. *clubb'd*] combined.

22. *old*] around sixty-five years old; according to a 1632 Deposition (Lyster *vs.* White) at London Public Records Office, Brome was forty-five or thereabouts in 1632 (Requests Proceedings, Chas. I., Bdl. 79, Pt. 1).

powder'd and ribboned wits of our days; but though I
cannot speak so much, I can think as well and as honorably
as the best. All the arguments I can use to induce you to take   25
notice of this thing of nothing is that it had the luck to
tumble last of all in the epidemical ruin of the scene, and
now limps hither with a wooden leg to beg an alms at your
hands. I will wind up all with a use of exhortation, that
since the times conspire to make us all beggars, let us make   30
ourselves merry; which (if I am not mistaken) this drives
at. Be pleased, therefore, sir, to lodge these harmless beggars
in the outhouses of your thoughts, and, among the rest, him,
that in this cuckoo time, puts in for a membership and
will fill the choir of those that "Duly and truly pray for you,"   35
and is,

Sir,

Your humble servant,

Richard Brome

26–27. *luck . . . last*] i.e., more than likely the last play performed at the
Cockpit before the closing of the theaters in 1642. See Introduction,
pp. xi–xii.

27. *epidemical*] general; a condition found everywhere.

34. *cuckoo time*] spring; also a time of usurpation by the Puritans, suggested by the bird's habit of laying its eggs in another bird's nest. Like
many dramatists of the time Brome allied himself with the Royalist cause.

35. *Duly . . . you*] See III.i.144 ff.

To Master Richard Brome, on his Play Called
A Jovial Crew: or, The Merry Beggars

Plays are instructive recreations,
Which, who would write may not expect, at once,
No, nor with every breeding, to write well.
And, though some itching academics fell
Lately upon this task, their products were 5
Lame and imperfect, and did grate the ear,
So that they mock'd the stupid stationer's care,
That both with gilt and cringes did prepare
Fine copper cuts, and gather'd verses, too,
To make a shout before the idle show. 10
 Your fate is other: you do not invade,
But by great Jonson were made free o'th' trade,
So that we must in this your labor find
Some image and fair relic of his mind.

JOHN HALL 15

To Master . . . *Beggars*] *not in Q3.*

---

4. *itching academics*] academic dramatists; e.g., Aston Cokain, John Denham, Nathaniel Richards, Sir Ralph Freeman, William Lowers, and Arthur Wilson. (See A. Harbage, *Cavalier Drama* [New York, 1936], pp. 127–136.)

 9. *Fine copper cuts*] elaborate frontispieces, engraved portraits.

 9–10. *gather'd . . . show*] An allusion to W. Cartwright's *Works* (edn. 1651) with its fifty-odd prefatory poems of commendation. Since the commendatory verses evidently came in and were set up piecemeal (see Greg, Vol. III), the number of poems varies in different copies.

 12. *Jonson . . . trade*] Brome was in the service of Ben Jonson in 1614. His name is first mentioned in Jonson's *Bartholomew Fair* as Jonson's "man, Master Brome"; Jonson addresses his commendatory verses prefixed to Brome's *The Northern Lasse* (edn. 1632) "To my old Faithfull Servant: and (by his continu'd Vertue) my Loving Friend: the Author of this Work, M. Rich. Brome": "I Had you for a Servant, once, Dick Brome;/ And you perform'd a Servants Faithfull parts." Jonson then commends Brome for his "observation of those Comick Lawes/ Which I, your Master, first did teach the Age./ You learn'd it well; and for it, serv'd your time/ A Prentise-ship; which few doe now a dayes."

 15. *John Hall*] (1627–1656), poet and pamphleteer, was the son of Michael Hall. He was admitted to St. John's College, Cambridge, and afterwards he entered Gray's Inn. Wood observes that "had not his debauchery and intemperance diverted him from the more serious studies, he had made an extraordinary person, for no man had ever done so great things at his age" (Wood's *Athenae*, ed. Bliss, II, 457–460, quoted in *DNB*). Awarded a pension by Cromwell for his pamphleteering service, he was held in high repute by his contemporaries. He was a friend of James Shirley and Thomas Stanley.

To Master Richard Brome, on his Comedy
of *A Jovial Crew: or, The Merry Beggars*

Not to commend or censure thee or thine,
Nor like a bush, to signify good wine,
Nor yet to publish to the world, or thee,
Thou merit'st bays by wit and poetry,
Do I stand here. Though I do know there comes   5
A shoal, with regiments of encomiums,
On all occasions, whose astronomy
Can calculate a praise to fifty-three,
And write blank copies, such as being view'd
May serve indifferently each altitude,   10
And make books, like petitions, whose commands
Are not from worth but multitude of hands;
Those will prove wit by power, and make a trade,
To force by number when they can't persuade.
Here's no such need, for books, like children, be   15
Well christen'd when their sureties are but three.
And those, which to twelve godfathers do come,
Signify former guilt, or speedy doom.
    Nor need the stationer, when all th' wits are past,
Bring his own periwig poetry at last.   20

To Master . . . Beggars] *not in Q 3.*

---

2. *bush . . . wine*] proverb: Good wine needs no bush (Tilley, W 462). The bush was a "branch or bunch of ivy (perhaps as the plant sacred to Bacchus) hung up as a vinter's sign" (*OED*).

6–8. *regiments . . . fifty-three*] another allusion to the commendatory poems in W. Cartwright's *Works* (edn. 1651); in the last poem "The Stationer to the Reader," H. Moseley calculates the number of contributors: "as many . . . as there are Shires in England, Weeks i' th' yeare, but actually fifty-three" (See Hall's verses above, ll. 9–10, note.)

16. *Well christen'd*] proverbial: "When the child is christened you may have godfathers enough" (Tilley, C 319).

17–18. *twelve . . . doom*] reference to the twelve men of a jury, jokingly called godfathers, who may condemn a man to death; cf. *Merchant of Venice*, IV.i.395 ff: "In christening thou shalt have two godfathers;/ Had I been judge, thou shouldst have had ten more,/ To bring thee to the gallows, not the font."

19–20. *stationer . . . last*] See above, ll. 6–8, note; a similar arrangement of poem and postscript by the stationer, Humphrey Mosley, following numerous commendatory poems is found in *Comedies and Tragedies Written by Francis Beaumont and John Fletcher Gentlemen*, edn. 1647.

To Master Richard Brome

All this won't do, for when their labor's done,
The reader's rul'd, not by their tastes, but's own.
And he, that for encomiastics looks,
May find the bigger, not the better books.
So that the most our leavers serve for, shows   25
Only that we're his friends, and do suppose
'Tis good; and that is all that I shall say.
In truth I love him well, and like his play.
And if there's any that don't think so, too,
Let them let it alone for them that do.   30

J. B.

---

31. *J. B.*] unidentified. The initials are assigned to one of the commendatory poems in Thomas Jordan's *Poetical Varieties* (edn. 1637), which also
contains commendatory verses by Brome.

To His Worthy Friend, Master Richard Brome,
Upon his Comedy Called
A Jovial Crew: or, The Merry Beggars

This comedy, ingenious friend, will raise
Itself a monument without a praise
Begg'd by the stationer, who, with strength of purse
And pens, takes care to make his book sell worse.
And I dare calculate thy play, although   5
Not elevated unto fifty-two,
It may grow old as time or wit, and he
That dares despise may after envy thee.
    Learning, the file of poesy, may be
Fetch'd from the arts and university;   10
But he that writes a play, and good, must know
Beyond his books, men and their actions, too.
Copies of verse, that make the new men sweat,
Reach not a poem, nor the muse's heat;
Small bavin wits and wood may burn awhile,   15

To His . . . *Beggars*] *not in Q3.*

---

4. *sell worse*] "worse" used "as an intensive," i.e., sell "in a greater degree" (*OED*). Humphrey Moseley, the publishing bookseller, begged commendatory poems from numerous contributors, seemingly to increase the sale of the book rather than to attest the author's (Cartwright's) worth. Cf. commendatory verses by J. B., ll. 13–14; Ben Jonson's Epigram III, "To my Booke-seller": "Thou, that mak'st gaine thy end, and wisely well,/ Call'st a booke good, or bad, as it doth sell" (*The Works of Ben Jonson*, edn. 1616, p. 769).

5–6. *calculate . . . fifty-two*] another allusion to Cartwright's *Works* (edn. 1651). (See Hall's verses above, ll. 9–10, note.)

9. *Learning . . . poesy*] i.e., through learning, one polishes and perfects poetry; cf. Caesar Ripa's *Iconologia* (edn. 1709, Fig. 2) where *Academia* is represented by "A Lady of a manly heroic Aspect," wearing a crown of gold and holding in her right hand a file and in her left a garland. The file denotes "the polishing of pieces, and freeing them from Superfluities."

13. *new men*] courtier and academic playwrights, such as William Strode, William Cartwright and Sir John Suckling, whose plays became popular for their elaborate masque staging.

15. *bavin wits*] i.e., inferior literary men who lack profundity. A *bavin* is a bundle of brushwood. Cf. proverb: "The Bavin burns bright but it is but a blaze" (Tilley, B 107), and Shakespeare's *Henry IV, Part I*: "Shallow jesters and rash bavin wits,/ Soon kindled and soon burnt" (III.ii.61).

And make more noise than forests on a pile,
Whose fibres shrunk, ma' invite a piteous stream,
Not to lament, but to extinguish them.
Thy fancy's metal, and thy strain's much higher
Proof 'gainst their wit and what that dreads, the fire.   20

JAMES SHIRLEY

17. fibres] *this edition;* Fivers *Q 1–2;
not in Q 3.*

19–20. *fancy's . . . fire*] i.e., Brome's imaginative faculty (his fancy), unlike that of inferior dramatists (*bavin wits,* l. 15), is not combustible.

21. *James Shirley*] (1596–1666), poet, playwright, born in London, educated at Merchant Taylors' School, St. John's College, Oxford, and Catherine Hall, Cambridge. He took orders soon after 1619 and later lived in Gray's Inn and "set up for a playmaker," writing most of his plays between 1626 and 1642.

To My Worthy Friend, Master Richard Brome,
on his Excellent Play Called
A Jovial Crew: or, The Merry Beggars

There is a faction, friend, in town, that cries,
Down with the dagon poet; Jonson dies.
His works were too elaborate, not fit
To come within the verge or face of wit.
Beaumont and Fletcher, they say, perhaps might   5
Pass well for current coin in a dark night;
But Shakespeare, the plebeian driller, was
Founder'd in's *Pericles*, and must not pass.
And so, at all men fly, that have but been
Thought worthy of applause; therefore, their spleen.   10
Ingrateful Negro-kind, dart you your rage
Against the beams that warm'd you, and the stage!
This malice shows it is unhallowed heat
That boils your raw brains, and your temples beat.
Adulterate pieces may retain the mold,   15
Or stamp, but want the pureness of the gold.
But the world's mad; those jewels that were worn
In high esteem by some, laid by in scorn,
Like Indians, who their native wealth despise,
And dote on stranger's trash and trumperies.   20
Yet if it be not too far spent, there is
Some hopes left us, that this, thy well-wrought piece,

To Master . . . *Beggars*] *not in Q3.*

---

2. *dagon poet*] in transferred sense, once an idol, but here, a term of
reproach (so *OED*).
    4. *verge*] "within an area subject to the jurisdiction of the Lord High
Steward, defined as extending to a distance of twelve miles round the
King's court" (*OED*).
    7. *driller*] interpretation ambiguous: (1) "one who entices or allures"
(*OED*); i.e., Shakespeare entices or allures those with plebeian tastes;
(2) one who "protracts" or "lengthens out" (*OED*); i.e., Shakespeare is
one who aimlessly protracts old tales like *Pericles*.
    8. *Founder'd in's Pericles*] Tatham alludes to the rambling nature of the
play and the complete indifference to Aristotelian principles of dramatic
structure espoused by disciples of Jonson.

May bring it cure, reduce it to its sight,
To judge th' difference 'twixt the day and night;
Draw th' curtain of their errors, that their sense   25
May be conformable to Ben's influence,
And finding here nature and art agree,
May swear, thou liv'st in him, and he in thee.

JOHN TATHAM

---

29. *John Tatham*] (fl. 1632–1664), dramatist and city poet, successor to John Taylor and Thomas Heywood as poet laureate to the Lord Mayor's show. He wrote city pageants regularly from 1657 to 1664 as well as a few plays. Among the commendatory verses in his *Fancies Theater* (edn. 1640) are those of Richard Brome.

To Master Richard Brome, upon his Comedy Called
A Jovial Crew: or, The Merry Beggars

Something I'd say, but not to praise thee, friend,
For thou thyself dost best thyself commend.
And he that with an eulogy doth come,
May to's own wit raise an encomium,
But not to thine. Yet I'll before thee go,   5
Though whiffler-like, to usher in the show.
And like a quarter-clock, foretell the time
Is come about for greater bells to chime.
　　I must not praise thy poetry nor wit,
Though both are very good; yet that's not it.   10
The reader in his progress will find more
Wit in a line than I praise in a score.
I shall be read with prejudice, for each line
I write of thee, or anything that's thine,
Be't name or muse, will all be read of me,   15
As if I claw'd myself by praising thee.
　　But though I may not praise, I hope I may
Be bold to love thee. And the world shall say
I've reason for't. I love thee for thy name;
I love thee for thy merit, and thy fame;   20
I love thee for thy neat and harmless wit,
Thy mirth that does so clean and closely hit.
Thy luck to please so well; who could go faster
At first to be the envy of thy master?
I love thee for thyself, for who can choose   25
But like the fountain of so brisk a muse?
I love this comedy, and every line,
Because 'tis good as well's because 'tis thine.

---

　　6. *whiffler*] "One of the body of attendants armed with a javelin, battle-axe, sword, or staff, and wearing a chain, employed to keep the way clear for a procession or at some public spectacle" (*OED*).
　　16. *claw'd*] flattered.
　　21. *neat*] cleverly contrived.
　　24. *envy of thy master*] Jonson's apparent pique occasioned by the success of Brome's *Lovesick Maid* at Blackfriars just a few weeks after the failure of Jonson's *The New Inn* in 1629 at the same theater is expressed in his *Ode to Himself*.

Thou tell'st the world the life that beggars lead;
'Tis seasonable, 'twill become our trade.   30
'T must be our study, too; for in this time
Who'll not be innocent, since wealth's a crime?
Thou'rt th'age's doctor now, for since all go
To make us poor, thou mak'st us merry too.
   Go on, and thrive; may all thy sportings be   35
Delightful unto all as th' are to me.
May this so please t'encourage thee, that more
May be made public, which thou keep'st in store.
That though we've lost their dress, we may be glad
To see and think on th' happiness we had.   40
   And thou thereby mayst make our name to shine;
'Twas royal once, but now 'twill be divine.

                                                 ALEXANDER BROME

---

42. *royal once*] A. W. Ward suggests that Alexander Brome is associating "Brome" with "Plantagenet" (*DNB*), i.e., *planta genesta*, the broom flower worn in the helmet of the first of the Plantaganet kings, Henry II.

42. *divine*] everlasting.

43. *Alexander Brome*] (1620–1660), poet, attorney in lord-mayor's court, dramatist, translator of *Leges Conviviales*, but no relative to Richard Brome. He was clerk to Peter Ball, a solicitor who sent him to Exeter College, Oxford; but he never took a degree. Listed among the friends of Jonson, he was one of the witty revelers at the Devil Tavern. During the Civil War he attached himself to the royalist cause. He edited the volumes of Brome's plays titled *Five New Plays* in 1653 and again in 1659. Because of his jovial disposition and spirited bacchanalian lyrics, he has been called the English Anacreon.

PROLOGUE

The title of our play, *A Jovial Crew,*
May seem to promise mirth, which were a new
And forc'd thing in these sad and tragic days
For you to find, or we express in plays.
We wish you then would change that expectation,   5
Since jovial mirth is now grown out of fashion.
Or much not to expect, for now it chances
Our comic writer, finding that romances
Of lovers through much travel and distress,
Till it be thought no power can redress   10
Th'afflicted wanderers, though stout chivalry
Lend all his aid for their delivery,
Till, lastly, some impossibility
Concludes all strife and makes a comedy—
Finding, he says, such stories bear the sway,   15
Near as he could, he has compos'd a play
Of fortune-tellers, damsels, and their squires,
Expos'd to strange adventures through the briers
Of love and fate. But why need I forestall
What shall so soon be obvious to you all,   20
But wish the dullness may make no man sleep,
Nor sadness of it any woman weep.

---

8. *romances*] Lavish courtly plays, with their elaborate scenes and impossible fables of platonic love, offered formidable competition among theaters for public favor; e.g., Thomas Killigrew's *Prisoners* (written between 1632 and 1635), William Cartwright's *Royal Slave* (acted 1636–1637), Lodowick Carlell's *Osmond* (acted *c.* 1622), William Habington's *Queen of Aragon* (acted *c.* 1640).

THE PERSONS OF THE PLAY

OLDRENTS, *an ancient esquire*
HEARTY, *his friend and merry companion, but a decay'd gentleman*
SPRINGLOVE, *steward to Master Oldrents*
VINCENT, ⎱ *two young gentlemen*   5
HILLIARD, ⎰
RANDALL, *a groom, servant to Oldrents*
MASTER SENTWELL ⎱ *friends to Justice Clack*
and two other Gentlemen ⎰
OLIVER, *the Justice's son*
MASTER CLACK, *the Justice himself*   10
MASTER TALLBOY, *lover to the Justice's niece*
MARTIN, *the Justice's clerk*
CHAPLAIN ⎫
USHER ⎪
BUTLER ⎬ *to Oldrents*
COOK ⎭   15
RACHEL ⎱ *Oldrents' daughters*
MERIEL ⎰
AMIE, *Justice Clack's niece*
AUTEM-MORT, *an old beggar woman*   20
PATRICO ⎫
SOLDIER ⎪
LAWYER ⎬ *four especial beggars*
COURTIER ⎭
SCRIBBLE, *their poet*   25
Divers other Beggers, Fiddlers, and Mutes

---

1. *Oldrents*] Whereas rents of farm lands increased threefold between the years 1600 and 1688, Oldrents generously allowed his tenants to continue the old rate. See Hearty's speech, I.i.80 ff.; hence the appellation "Old Rents."

20. *Autem-Mort*] in canting language, a married woman (*Belman*, sig. El^v); Harman explains: "For Autem in their language is a Church, so shee is a wyfe married at the Church" (sig. F1^v).

21. *Patrico*] the hedge-priest of the gipsies: "Every hedge being his Parish, every wandring Harlot and Rogue his Parishioners, the service he sayes, is onely the marrying of couples, which hee does in a wood under a tree, or in the open field . . ." (*Belman*, sig. D4).

A Jovial Crew: or,
The Merry Beggars

[I.i]   [*Enter*] Oldrents, Hearty.

OLDRENTS.

It has indeed, friend, much afflicted me.

HEARTY.

And very justly, let me tell you, sir,
That could so impiously be curious
To tempt a judgment on you, to give ear,
And faith, too (by your leave), to fortune-tellers,   5
Wizards and gypsies!

OLDRENTS.   I have since been frighted
With't in a thousand dreams.

HEARTY.   I would be drunk
A thousand times to bed, rather than dream
Of any of their riddlemy riddlemies.
If they prove happy, so; if not, let't go;   10
You'll never find their meaning till the event,
If you suppose there was at all a meaning,
As the equivocating devil had when he
Cozen'd the monk to let him live soul-free

7. With't] *Q1–2;* with it *Q3.*

---

3. *curious*] anxious, concerned.
6. *Wizards*] commonly called wise men and wise women.
6. *gypsies*] John Minsheu, in *The Guide into Tongues* (edn. 1617), s.v.
"a counterfet Egyptian . . . or cousening/ Fortune-teller," explains:
"Egyptians are in our Statutes and Lawes of England, a counterfet kinde of
roagues, that being English or Welsh people, accompanie themselves together, disguising themselves in strange roabes, blacking their faces and
bodies, and framing to themselves an unknowen language, wander up and
downe, and under pretense of telling of fortunes, curing diseases, and such
like, abuse the ignorant common people, by stealing all that is not too hot,
or too heavie for their carriage."
9. *riddlemy riddlemies*] rigamarole; nonsense.

Till he should find him sleeping between sheets;   15
The wary monk, abjuring all such lodging,
At last, by over-watching in his study,
The foul fiend took him napping with his nose
Betwixt the sheet leaves of his conjuring book.
There was the whim, or double meaning on't.   20
But these fond fortune-tellers, that know nothing,
Aim to be thought more cunning than their master,
The foresaid devil, tho' truly not so hurtful.
Yet, trust 'em! Hang 'em. Wizards! Old blind buzzards!
For once they hit, they miss a thousand times;   25
And most times give quite contrary, bad for good,
And best for worst. Once told a gentleman
His son should be a man killer and hang'd for't;
Who after prov'd a great and rich physician,
And with great fame i'th' university   30
Hang'd up in picture for a grave example.
There was the whim of that. Quite contrary!

OLDRENTS.
And that was happy; would mine could so deceive my fears.

HEARTY.
They may, but trust not to't. Another schemist
Found that a squint-ey'd boy should prove a notable   35
Pickpurse, and afterwards a most strong thief;
When he grew up to be a cunning lawyer,
And at last died a judge. Quite contrary!
How many have been mark'd out by these wizards
For fools, that after have been prick'd for sheriffs?   40

---

20. *whim*] "a pun or play on words; a double meaning" (*OED*). This particular use of the word is found only in Brome, and is so used throughout the play.

21. *fond*] foolish.

22. *cunning*] possessing more magical knowledge or skill.

24–25. *Old . . . times*] *buzzard*, a name applied to "a worthless, stupid, or ignorant person" as well as to "an inferior kind of hawk, useless for falconry" (*OED*).

34. *schemist*] "a framer of 'schemes' or horoscopes; an astrologer" (*OED*).

35. *squint-ey'd*] double-dealing.

40. *prick'd for sheriffs*] "To mark (a name, or an item) in a list by making a 'prick' through or against it . . .; *spec.* (of a sovereign) to select (persons) for the office of sheriff from a list by this means" (*OED*).

Was not a shepherd boy foretold to be
A drunkard, and to get his living from
Bawds, whores, thieves, quarrelers, and the like?
And did he not become a suburb justice?
And live in wine and worship by the fees   45
Rack'd out of such delinquents? There's the whim on't.
Now I come to you: your figure-flinger finds
That both your daughters, notwithstanding all
Your great possessions, which they are coheirs of,
Shall yet be beggars. May it not be meant   50
(If, as I said, there be a meaning in it),
They may prove courtiers, or great courtiers' wives,
And so be beggars in law? Is not that
The whim on't, think you? You shall think no worse on't.

OLDRENTS.
Would I had your merry heart.

HEARTY.   I thank you, sir.   55

OLDRENTS.
I mean the like.

HEARTY.   I would you had; and I
Such an estate as yours. Four thousand yearly,
With such a heart as mine, would defy fortune
And all her babbling soothsayers. I'd as soon
Distrust in providence as lend a fear   60
To such a destiny for a child of mine,
While there be sack and songs in town or country.
Think like a man of conscience (now I am serious),
What justice can there be for such a curse
To fall upon your heirs? Do you not live   65
Free, out of law, or grieving any man?
Are you not th' only rich man lives unenvied?
Have you not all the praises of the rich,
And prayers of the poor? Did ever any
Servant, or hireling, neighbor, kindred curse you,   70
Or wish one minute shorten'd of your life?
Have you one grudging tenant? Will they not all

---

46. *Rack'd*] extorted.
47. *figure-flinger*] pretender to astrology.
53. *beggars in law*] nonce variant of statute beggars. See note to II.i.166.

Fight for you? Do they not teach their children,
And make 'em, too, pray for you morn and evening,
And in their graces, too, as duly as   75
For king and realm? The innocent things would think
They ought not eat else.

OLDRENTS.   'Tis their goodness.

HEARTY.

It is your merit. Your great love and bounty
Procures from Heaven those inspirations in 'em.
Whose rent did ever you exact? Whose have   *generous*
You not remitted, when by casualties   *landlord* – 80
Of fire, of floods, of common dearth, or sickness,
Poor men were brought behindhand? Nay, whose losses
Have you not piously repair'd?

OLDRENTS.   Enough.

HEARTY.

What heriots have you ta'en from forlorn widows?   85
What acre of your thousands have you rack'd?

OLDRENTS.

Good friend, no more.

HEARTY.   These are enough, indeed,
To fill your ears with joyful acclamations
Where'er you pass: "Heaven bless our Landlord Oldrents,
Our Master Oldrents, our good Patron Oldrents."   90
Cannot these sounds conjure that evil spirit
Of fear out of you, that your children shall
Live to be beggars? Shall Squire Oldrents' daughters
Wear old rents in their garments (there's a whim, too),
Because a fortune-teller told you so?   95

OLDRENTS.

Come, I will strive to think no more on't.

HEARTY.

Will you ride forth for air then, and be merry?

83. losses] *Q2–3; not in Q1.*

---

85. *heriots*] "a render of the best live beast or dead chattel of a deceased
tenant due by legal custom to the lord of whom he held; . . . At an early
period this render was commuted in many cases for a fixed money payment"
(*OED*).
86. *rack'd*] charged "an excessive rent for land" (*OED*).

OLDRENTS.

Your counsel and example may instruct me.

HEARTY.

Sack must be had in sundry places, too.

For songs I am provided.   100

Enter Springlove *with books and papers; he lays them on the table.*

OLDRENTS.

Yet here comes one brings me a second fear,

Who has my care the next unto my children.

HEARTY.

Your steward, sir, it seems has business with you.

I wish you would have none.

OLDRENTS.   I'll soon dispatch it,

And then be for our journey instantly.   105

HEARTY.

I'll wait your coming down, sir.   *Exit.*

OLDRENTS.   But why, Springlove,

Is now this expedition?

SPRINGLOVE.   Sir, 'tis duty.

OLDRENTS.

Not common among stewards, I confess,

To urge in their accompts before the day

Their lords have limited. Some that are grown   110

To hoary hairs and knighthoods are not found

Guilty of such an importunity.

'Tis yet but thirty days, when I give forty

After the half-year day, our Lady last.

Could I suspect my trust were lost in thee,   115

Or doubt thy youth had not ability

---

102. the] *Q1–2; not in Q3.*   106. S.D. *Exit*] *Q1–2; not in Q3.*

---

107. *expedition*] promptitude.

109. *accompts*] accounts.

112. *importunity*] i.e., Springlove's persistent endeavors to hand in the account ahead of time.

114. *Lady last*] The accounting year usually began on Michaelmas Day, the half-yearly accounts being closed on Lady Day, or March 25. Springlove presents his accounts only thirty days after the half-year day, or April 25, though he was allowed forty days, or until about May 5.

To carry out the weight of such a charge,
I, then, should call on thee.
SPRINGLOVE.   Sir, your indulgence,
I hope, shall ne'er corrupt me. Ne'ertheless,
The testimony of a fair discharge   120
From time to time will be encouragement

    Springlove turns over the several books to his master.

To virtue in me. You may then be pleas'd
To take here a survey of all your rents
Receiv'd, and all such other payments as
Came to my hands since my last audit, for   125
Cattle, wool, corn, all fruits of husbandry.
Then my receipts on bonds, and some new leases,
With some old debts, and almost desperate ones,
As well from country cavaliers as courtiers.
Then here, sir, are my several disbursements   130
In all particulars for yourself and daughters,
In charge of housekeeping, buildings and repairs;
Journeys, apparel, coaches, gifts, and all
Expenses for your personal necessaries.
Here, servants' wages, liveries, and cures.   135
Here for supplies of horses, hawks and hounds.
And lastly, not the least to be remember'd,
Your large benevolences to the poor.
OLDRENTS.
Thy charity there goes hand in hand with mine.
And, Springlove, I commend it in thee, that   140
So young in years art grown so ripe in goodness.
May their Heaven-piercing prayers bring on thee
Equal rewards with me.
SPRINGLOVE.   Now here, sir, is
The balance of the several accompts,
Which shows you what remains in cash: which added   145
Unto your former bank, makes up in all—

127. on] *Q1;* and *Q2–3.*   138. benevolences] *Q1;* benevo-
135–136.] *lines inverted Q3.*   lence *Q2–3.*

   128. *desperate*] irretrievable.
   135. *cures*] medical treatments.
   146. *bank*] sum of money.

OLDRENTS.
Twelve thousand and odd pounds.
SPRINGLOVE.   Here are the keys
Of all. The chests are safe in your own closet.
OLDRENTS.
Why in my closet? Is not yours as safe?
SPRINGLOVE.
Oh, sir, you know my suit.
OLDRENTS.   Your suit? What suit?   150
SPRINGLOVE.
Touching the time of year.
OLDRENTS.   'Tis well-nigh May.
Why what of that, good Springlove?

Nightingale sings.

SPRINGLOVE.
Oh, sir, you hear I am call'd.
OLDRENTS.   Fie, Springlove, fie.
I hop'd thou hadst abjur'd that uncouth practice.
SPRINGLOVE.
You thought I had forsaken nature then.   155
OLDRENTS.
Is that disease of nature still in thee
So virulent? And notwithstanding all
My favors in my gifts, my cares, and counsels,
Which to a soul ingrateful might be boasted;
Have I first bred thee, and then preferr'd thee (from   160
I will not say how wretched a beginning)
To be a master over all my servants,
Planted thee in my bosom, and canst thou,
There, slight me for the whistling of a bird?
SPRINGLOVE.
Your reason, sir, informs you, that's no cause.   165
But 'tis the season of the year that calls me.
What moves her notes provokes my disposition
By a more absolute power of nature than
Philosophy can render an accompt for.

---

149. *closet*] a private chamber.

OLDRENTS.

I find there's no expelling it, but still   170
It will return. I have tried all the means
(As I may safely think) in human wisdom,
And did (as near as reason could) assure me,
That thy last year's restraint had stopp'd forever
That running sore on thee, that gadding humor;   175
When, only for that cause, I laid the weight
Of mine estate in stewardship upon thee,
Which kept thee in that year, after so many
Summer vagaries thou hadst made before.

SPRINGLOVE.

You kept a swallow in a cage that while.   180
I cannot, sir, endure another summer
In that restraint, with life; 'twas then my torment,
But now, my death. Yet, sir, my life is yours,
Who are my patron; freely may you take it.
Yet pardon, sir, my frailty, that do beg   185
A small continuance of it on my knees.

OLDRENTS.

Can there no means be found to preserve life
In thee but wand'ring like a vagabond?
Does not the sun as comfortably shine
Upon my gardens as the opener fields?   190
Or on my fields, as others far remote?
Are not my walks and greens as delectable
As the highways and commons? Are the shades
Of sycamore and bowers of eglantine
Less pleasing than of bramble or thorn hedges?   195
Or of my groves and thickets, than wild woods?
Are not my fountain waters fresher than
The troubled streams, where every beast does drink?
Do not the birds sing here as sweet and lively
As any other where? Is not thy bed more soft,   200
And rest more safe, than in a field or barn?
Is a full table, which is call'd thine own,

---

179. *vagaries*] wanderings.
180. *swallow*] i.e., Springlove, like the swallow, by nature is "the most
perfect herald of the Spring" (Phillips, p. 191).

Less curious or wholesome than the scraps
From others' trenchers, twice or thrice translated?
SPRINGLOVE.

Yea, in the winter season, when the fire   205
Is sweeter than the air.
OLDRENTS.   What air is wanting?
SPRINGLOVE.

Oh, sir, y'have heard of pilgrimages, and
The voluntary travels of good men.
OLDRENTS.

For penance, or to holy ends? But bring
Not those into comparison, I charge you.   210
SPRINGLOVE.

I do not, sir. But pardon me, to think
Their sufferings are much sweetened by delights,
Such as we find by shifting place and air.
OLDRENTS.

Are there delights in beggary? Or, if to take
Diversity of air be such a solace,   215
Travel the kingdom over; and if this
Yield not variety enough, try further,
Provided your deportment be gentle.
Take horse, and man, and money; you have all,
Or I'll allow enough.

Sing nightingale, cuckoo, &c.

SPRINGLOVE.   Oh how am I confounded!   220
Dear sir, retort me naked to the world
Rather than lay those burdens on me which
Will stifle me. I must abroad or perish.
OLDRENTS.

I will no longer strive to wash this Moor,
Nor breathe more minutes so unthriftily   225
In civil argument against rude wind,

---

203. *curious*] exquisitely prepared.
221. *retort*] "to cast or throw (one) out" (*OED*).
224. *wash this Moor*] variation of "To wash an Ethiop," thus to attempt
an impossible task.

But rather practice to withdraw my love
And tender care (if it be possible)
From that unfruitful breast, incapable
Of wholesome counsel.

SPRINGLOVE.   Have I your leave, sir?   230

OLDRENTS.
    I leave you to dispute it with yourself.
    I have no voice to bid you go or stay;
    My love shall give thy will pre-eminence,
    And leave th'effect to time and providence.   *Exit.*

SPRINGLOVE.
    I am confounded in my obligation   235
    To this good man: his virtue is my punishment,
    When 'tis not in my nature to return
    Obedience to his merits. I could wish
    Such an ingratitude were death by th' law,
    And put in present execution on me   240
    To rid me of my sharper suffering.
    Nor but by death can this predominant sway
    Of nature be extinguish'd in me. I
    Have fought with my affections, by th'assistance
    Of all the strengths of art and discipline   245
    (All which I owe him for in education, too)
    To conquer and establish my observance
    (As in all other rules) to him in this,
    This inborn strong desire of liberty
    In that free course, which he detests as shameful,   250
    And I approve my earth's felicity;
    But find the war is endless, and must fly.
    What must I lose then? A good master's love.
    What loss feels he that wants not what he loses?
    They'll say I lose all reputation.   255
    What's that, to live where no such thing is known?
    My duty to a master will be question'd.
    Where duty is exacted, it is none,
    And among beggars, each man is his own.

---

245. *art and discipline*] learning and instruction.
258. *duty*] i.e., reverence (Onions).

Enter Randall *and three or four servants with a great kettle, and black jacks, and a baker's basket, all empty; exeunt with all; manet* Randall.

Now fellows, what news from whence you came?   260

RANDALL.

The old wonted news, sir, from your guesthouse, the old barn. We have unloaden the breadbasket, the beef kettle, and the beer bumbards there amongst your guests, the beggars. And they have all prayed for you and our master, as their manner is, from the teeth outward. Marry, from 265 the teeth inwards, 'tis enough to swallow your alms, from whence I think their prayers seldom come.

SPRINGLOVE.

Thou should'st not think uncharitably.

RANDALL.

Thought's free, Master Steward, and it please you. But your charity is nevertheless notorious, I must needs say.   270

SPRINGLOVE.

Meritorious, thou meant'st to say.

RANDALL.

Surely, sir, no; 'tis out of our curate's book.

SPRINGLOVE.

But I aspire no merits, nor popular thanks; 'tis well if I do well in it.

RANDALL.

It might be better though (if old Randall, whom you allow 275 to talk, might counsel) to help to breed up poor men's children, or decayed laborers, past their work, or travail; or towards the setting up of poor, young married couples, than to bestow an hundred pound a year (at least you do that, if not all you get), besides your master's bounty, 280 to maintain in begging such wanderers as these, that never

280. your] *Coxeter;* our *Q1–3.*

259.1. *black jacks*] leather vessels for liquor, coated outside with tar or pitch.

263. *beer bumbards*] large cans or vessels for holding beer.

265. *teeth outward*] sincerity only feigned, not from the heart.

269. *Thought's free*] proverbial: Tilley, T 244.

270. *notorious*] "Such as is or may be generally, openly, or publicly known" (*OED*), as well as the more unfavorable sense of the word.

are out of their way; that cannot give account from whence *no social place.*
they came or whither they would; nor of any beginning they
ever had, or any end they seek, but still to stroll and
beg till their bellies be full, and then sleep till they be 285
hungry.

SPRINGLOVE.

Thou art ever repining at those poor people! They take
nothing from thee but thy pains, and that I pay thee for,
too. Why should'st thou grudge?

RANDALL.

Am I not bitten to it every day, by the six-footed blood- 290
hounds that they leave in their litter, when I throw out
the old to lay fresh straw for the newcomers at night.
That's one part of my office. And you are sure that, though
your hospitality be but for a night and a morning for one
rabble, to have a new supply every evening. They take 295
nothing from me indeed; they give too much.

SPRINGLOVE.

Thou art old Randall still! Ever grumbling, but still
officious for 'em.

RANDALL.

Yes, hang 'em; they know I love 'em well enough. I have
had merry bouts with some of 'em.   300

SPRINGLOVE.

What say'st thou, Randall?

RANDALL.

They are indeed my pastime. I left the merry grigs (as their *Vagabond entertainers!*
provender has prick'd 'em) in such a hoigh yonder! Such a
frolic! You'll hear anon as you walk nearer 'em.

SPRINGLOVE.

Well, honest Randall, thus it is. I am for a journey. I know 305
not how long will be my absence. But I will presently take

284. to] *Q1;* do *Q2–3.*

290–291. *six-footed blood-hounds*] fleas and lice.
300. *bouts*] i.e., drinking bouts.
302. *grigs*] "an extravagantly lively person, one who is full of frolic and
jest" (*OED*).
303. *provender . . . 'em*] i.e., as food and drink has made them high-spirited.
303. *hoigh*] excitement, riot.

order with the cook, pantler and butler for my wonted
allowance to the poor; and I will leave money with thee to
manage the affair till my return.

RANDALL.

Then up rise Randall, bailie of the beggars.   310

SPRINGLOVE.

And if our master shall be displeas'd (although the charge
be mine) at the openness of the entertainment, thou shalt
then give it proportionably in money and let them walk
farther.

RANDALL.

Pseugh! That will never do't, never do 'em good. 'Tis the 315
seat, the habitation, the rendezvous that cheers their hearts.
<u>Money would clog their consciences.</u> Nor must I lose the
music of 'em in their lodging.

SPRINGLOVE.

We will agree upon't anon. Go now about your business.

RANDALL.

I go. Bailie? Nay, steward and chamberlain of the rogues 320
and beggars.   *Exit.*

SPRINGLOVE.

I cannot think but with a trembling fear
On this adventure, in a scruple which
I have not weighed with all my other doubts.
I shall in my departure rob my master.   325
Of what? Of a true servant; other theft
I have committed none. And that may be supplied,
And better, too, by some more constant to him.
But I may injure many in his trust,
Which now he cannot be but sparing of.   330
I rob him, too, of the content and hopes
He had in me, whom he had built and rais'd
Unto that growth in his affection

333. that] *Q1*; what *Q2–3*.

---

307. *pantler*] alteration of "panter," originally meaning "baker" but later
applied to one in charge of the pantry in a household.
310. *bailie*] "bailiff" or "chief magistrate" (*OED*).
312. *openness*] open-handedness.
320. *chamberlain*] high steward or factor of a nobleman.

That I became a gladness in his eye,
And now must be a grief or a vexation   335

A noise and singing within.

Unto his noble heart. But hark! Ay, there's
The harmony that drowns all doubts and fears.
A little nearer—

SONG

From hunger and cold, who lives more free,
 Or who more richly clad than we?   340
Our bellies are full; our flesh is warm;
 And, against pride, our rags are a charm.
Enough is our feast, and for tomorrow
Let rich men care; we feel no sorrow.
 No sorrow, no sorrow, no sorrow, no sorrow.   345
 Let rich men care; we feel no sorrow

SPRINGLOVE.
The emperor hears no such music, nor feels content like this!

[SONG]

Each city, each town, and every village,
 Affords us either an alms or pillage.
And if the weather be cold and raw   350
 Then, in a barn we tumble in straw.
If warm and fair, by yea-cock and nay-cock
 The fields will afford us a hedge or a haycock.
 A haycock, a haycock, a haycock, a haycock,
 The fields will afford us a hedge or a haycock.   355

SPRINGLOVE.
Most ravishing delight! But in all this
Only one sense is pleas'd: mine ear is feasted.
Mine eye, too, must be satisfied with my joys.
The hoarding usurer cannot have more

339–346.] The tune and words are printed in *Select Ayres and Dialogues,
for One, Two, and Three Voyces* (edn. 1669), p. 64.
 351–352. *tumble . . . yea-cock*] "By cock" is a form of oath, a euphemism
for "By God"; possible pun: 1) prognostication of a weathercock, 2)
copulating in the straw (Partridge, p. 88). Cf. III.i.96, note.

Thirsty desire to see his golden store   360
When he unlocks his treasury than I
The equipage in which my beggars lie.

He opens the scene; the Beggars *are discovered in their postures; then they*
issue forth; and last, the Patrico.

ALL.

Our master, our master! Our sweet and comfortable master.

SPRINGLOVE.

How cheer my hearts?

1 BEGGAR.   Most crouse, most cap'ringly.
Shall we dance, shall we sing, to welcome our king?   365
Strike up piper a merry, merry dance
That we on our stampers may foot it and prance,
To make his heart merry as he has made ours,
As lustic and frolic as lords in their bowers.

Music. Dance.

SPRINGLOVE.

Exceeding well perform'd.   370

1 BEGGAR.

'Tis well if it like you, master. But we have not that rag
among us that we will not dance off to do you service; we
being all and only your servants, most noble sir. Command
us, therefore, and employ us, we beseech you.

SPRINGLOVE.

Thou speak'st most courtly.   375

2 BEGGAR.

Sir, he can speak, and could have writ as well. He is a
decay'd poet, newly fallen in among us, and begs as well
as the best of us. He learn'd it pretty well in his own
profession before, and can the better practice it in ours
now.   380

362.1. *opens the scene*] draws the curtains to inner stage.
362.1. *postures*] various poses or attitudes related to beggar conditions.
363. *comfortable*] pleasant, enjoyable.
364. *crouse*] in "lively spirits" (*OED*).
367. *stampers*] shoes (*Lanthorne*, sig. C3).
369. *lustic*] merry, jolly; chiefly with reference to drink (*OED*).

SPRINGLOVE.

Thou art a wit, too, it seems.

3 BEGGAR.

He should have wit and knavery, too, sir, for he was an
attorney, till he was pitch'd over the bar. And from that
fall he was taken up a knight o'the post, and so he continued
till he was degraded at the whipping post, and from thence 385
he ran resolutely into this course. His cunning in the law,
and the other's labor with the muses, are dedicate to your
service; and for myself, I'll fight for you.

SPRINGLOVE.

Thou art a brave fellow, and speak'st like a commander.
Hast thou borne arms?   390

4 BEGGAR.

Sir, he has borne the name of a Netherland soldier till he
ran away from his colors, and was taken lame with lying in
the fields by a sciatica; I mean, sir, the strappado. After
which, by a second retreat, indeed running away, he
scambled into this country, and so 'scap'd the gallows; and 395
then snapp'd up his living in the city by his wit in cheating,
pimping, and such like arts, till the cart and the pillory
showed him too publicly to the world. And so, begging
being the last refuge, he enter'd into our society. And
now lives honestly, I must needs say, as the best of us.   400

SPRINGLOVE.

Thou speak'st good language, too.

395. this] *Coxeter;* his *Q 1–3.*

383. *pitch'd . . . bar*] disbarred.
384. *knight o'the post*] "one who got his living by giving false evidence"
(*OED*).
393. *strappado*] A method of torture; see Coryat's *Crudities* (edn. 1611,
p. 254): "I saw . . . two men tormented with the strapado, which is done
in this manner. The offendor having his hands bound behind him, is
conveighed into a rope that hangeth in a pully, and after hoysed up in the
rope to a great height with two severall swinges, where he sustaineth so
great torments that his joynts are for the time loosed and pulled asunder;
besides such abundance of bloud is gathered into his hands and face, that
for the time he is in the torture, his face and hands doe looke as red as fire."
395. *scambled*] stumbled along.
397. *cart*] The carting of vagrants, bawds, and whores to the place of
punishment where they were publicly whipped is often alluded to in seventeenth-century literature.

1 BEGGAR.

He was a courtier born, sir, and begs on pleasure, I assure
you, refusing great and constant means from able friends to
make him a staid man. Yet (the want of a leg notwithstanding) he must travel in this kind against all common 405
reason, by the special policy of providence.

SPRINGLOVE.

As how, I prithee?

1 BEGGAR.

His father, sir, was a courtier, a great court beggar, I assure
you; I made these verses of him and his son here.

A courtier begg'd by covetise, not need,   410
From others that which made them beg indeed.
He begg'd till wealth had laden him with cares
To keep for's children and their children shares,
While the oppress'd, that lost that great estate,
Sent curses after it unto their fate.   415
The father dies (the world says) very rich;
The son, being gotten while (it seems) the itch
Of begging was upon the courtly sire,
Or bound by fate, will to no wealth aspire,
Though offer'd him in money, clothes or meat,   420
More than he begs, or instantly must eat.
Is not he heavenly blest, that hates earth's treasure
And begs, with "What's a gentleman but's pleasure?"
Or say it be upon the heir a curse,
What's that to him? The beggar's ne'er the worse.   425
For of the general store that Heaven has sent,
He values not a penny till't be spent.

ALL.

A scribble, a scribble!

2 BEGGAR.

What city or court poet could say more than our hedge
muse-monger here?   430

3 BEGGAR.

What say, sir, to our poet Scribble here?

431. S.P. 3 Beggar] *Coxeter;* 2 Beg.
Q 1–3.

___

404. *staid*] settled.

SPRINGLOVE.

I like his vein exceeding well; and the whole consort of you.

2 BEGGAR.

Consort, sir! We have musicians, too, among us: true merry
beggars indeed, that being within the reach of the lash for
singing libelous songs at London, were fain to fly into our 435
covey, and here they sing all our poet's ditties. They
can sing anything most tunably, sir, but Psalms. What they
may do hereafter under a triple tree is much expected. But
they live very civilly and gently among us.

SPRINGLOVE.

But what is he there, that solemn old fellow that neither 440
speaks of himself nor anybody for him?

2 BEGGAR.

Oh, sir, the rarest man of all. He is a prophet. See how he
holds up his prognosticating nose. He is divining now.

SPRINGLOVE.

How? A prophet?

2 BEGGAR.

Yes, sir, a cunning man and a fortune-teller. 'Tis thought 445
he was a great clerk before his decay, but he is very close,
will not tell his beginning, nor the fortune he himself is
fall'n from. But he serves us for a clergyman still, and
marries us, if need be, after a new way of his own.

SPRINGLOVE.

How long have you had his company?   450

2 BEGGAR.

But lately come amongst us, but a very ancient stroll-all-
the-land-over, and has travell'd with gypsies and is a patrico.
Shall he read your fortune, sir?

SPRINGLOVE.

If it please him.

PATRICO.

Lend me your hand, sir.   455

---

432. *consort*] pun: 1) fellowship and concord found among the crew;
2) musicians.

438. *triple tree*] gallows.

446. *close*] secretive.

By this palm I understand,
Thou art born to wealth and land,
And after many a bitter gust,
Shalt build with thy great grandsire's dust.

SPRINGLOVE.

Where shall I find it? But come, I'll not trouble my head   460
with the search.

2 BEGGAR.

What say, sir, to our crew? Are we not well congregated?

SPRINGLOVE.

You are a jovial crew, the only people
Whose happiness I admire.

3 BEGGAR.

Will you make us happy in serving you? Have you any   465
enemies? Shall we fight under you? Will you be our captain?

2 BEGGAR.

Nay, our king.

3 BEGGAR.

Command us something, sir.

SPRINGLOVE.

Where's the next rendezvous?

1 BEGGAR.

Neither in village nor in town,   470
But three mile off at Mapledown.

SPRINGLOVE.

At evening there I'll visit you.

SONG

Come, come; away: the spring
(By every bird that can but sing,

460. head] *Q1–2;* self *Q3.*

---

458. *gust*] a blast of wind.
471. *Mapledown*] located in Kent, on the north-west side of Wrotham
(Sugden).
473–492.] Brome and Coxeter (see List of Abbreviations) substitute a
song beginning "Courtiers, Courtiers, think it no Scorn" for the original
song. The original music under the title "The Beggar's Delight" is printed
in *Wit and Mirth, or Pills to Purge Melancholy*, IV (edn. 1719), p. 142.

Or chirp a note) doth now invite   475
Us forth, to taste of his delight.
In field, in grove, on hill, in dale;
But above all the nightingale,
Who in her swettness strives t'out-do
The loudness of the hoarse cuckoo.   480
"Cuckoo," cries he, "Jug, jug, jug," sings she,
From bush to bush, from tree to tree,
Why in one place then tarry we?

Come away; why do we stay?
We have no debt or rent to pay.   485
No bargains or accounts to make;
Nor land or lease to let or take:
Or if we had, should that remore us,
When all the world's our own before us,
And where we pass, and make resort,   490
It is our kingdom and our court.
"Cuckoo," cries he, &c.   *Exeunt* Cantantes.

SPRINGLOVE.
   So, now away.
   They dream of happiness that live in state,
   But they enjoy it that obey their fate.   495

[II.i]   [*Enter*] Vincent, Hilliard, Meriel, Rachel.

VINCENT.
   I am overcome with admiration at the felicity they take!

HILLIARD.
   Beggars! They are the only people can boast the benefit of a
   free state, in the full enjoyment of liberty, mirth and ease,
   having all things in common and nothing wanting of
   nature's whole provision within the reach of their desires.   5
   Who would have lost this sight of their revels?

VINCENT.
   How think you, ladies? Are they not the only happy in a
   nation?

---

488. *remore*] "To hinder, delay" (a rare word recorded only for *A Jovial
Crew* in *OED*).
   492. S.D. *Cantantes*] singers, from Latin *cantare* (to sing). For association
with *canters* (beggars), see II.i.213, note.

MERIEL.

Happier than we, I'm sure, that are pent up and tied by the
nose to the continual steam of hot hospitality here in our   10
father's house, when they have the air at pleasure in all
variety.

RACHEL.

And though I know we have merrier spirits than they, yet to
live thus confin'd, stifles us.

HILLIARD.

Why, ladies, you have liberty enough, or may take what you   15
please.

MERIEL.

Yes, in our father's rule and government, or by his allowance. What's that to absolute freedom, such as the very
beggars have, to feast and revel here today, and yonder
tomorrow, next day where they please, and so on still, the   20
whole country or kingdom over? There's liberty! The
birds of the air can take no more.

RACHEL.

And then at home here, or wheresoever he comes, our father
is so pensive (what muddy spirit soe'er possesses him,
would I could conjure't out) that he makes us even sick   25
of his sadness, that were wont to see my gossip's cock today,
mold cocklebread, dance clutterdepouch, and hannykin
booby, bind barrels, or do anything before him and he would
laugh at us.

MERIEL.

Now he never looks upon us but with a sigh, or tears in   30
his eyes, tho' we simper never so sanctifiedly. What tales

---

24. *muddy*] gloomy.
26. *gossip's*] "A familiar acquaintance, friend, chum"; here the reference
is apparently to "the name of some rustic game or dance" (*OED*).
27. *mold cocklebread*] a term probably derived from "cockly," or "cockle-
ty," moving to and fro. "Young wenches have a wanton sport which they
call moulding of cockle-bread, viz. they get upon a table-board, and then
gather up their knees and their coates with their hands as high as they can,
and then they wabble to and fro, as if they were kneading of dough, and
say these words, viz. My dame is sick and gonne to bed, And I'le go mould
my Cockle-bread" (quoted under a. 1697, *OED*).
27. *clutterdepouch*] an old dance.
27–28. *hannykin booby*] an old dance.
31. *sanctifiedly*] innocently.

have been told him of us, or what he suspects, I know not;
God forgive him, I do; but I am weary of his house.

RACHEL.

Does he think us whores, trow, because sometimes we talk as
lightly as great ladies. I can swear safely for the virginity   35
of one of us, so far as word and deed goes; marry, thought's
free.

MERIEL.

Which is that one of us, I pray? Yourself or me?

RACHEL.

Good sister Meriel, charity begins at home. But I'll swear
I think as charitably of thee, and not only because thou   40
art a year younger neither.

MERIEL.

I am beholden to you. But for my father, I would I knew
his grief and how to cure him, or that we were where we
could not see it. It spoils our mirth, and that has been
better than his meat to us.   45

VINCENT.

Will you hear our motion, ladies?

MERIEL.

Psew, you would marry us presently out of his way, because
he has given you a foolish kind of promise. But we will
see him in a better humor first, and as apt to laugh as we
to lie down, I warrant him.   50

HILLIARD.

'Tis like that course will cure him, would you embrace it.

RACHEL.

We will have him cur'd first, I tell you; and you shall
wait that season, and our leisure.

MERIEL.

I will rather hazard my being one of the devil's ape leaders,
than to marry while he is melancholy.   55

40. I think] *Q 1–2; not in Q 3.*

---

34. *trow*] do you believe.

39. *charity . . . home*] proverbial: Tilley, C 251.

49–50. *apt . . . lie down*] allusion to "Laugh and lay (lie) down," an
obsolete card game, and also to matrimony (Tilley, L 92).

54. *devil's ape leaders*] "To the mediaeval mind, every woman's destiny
was marriage. She could become the bride of man or the bride of God;
and if she wilfully rejected both these alternatives, she was warned that
after death her lot would be to lead apes in (or into) hell" (*Sh. Eng.*, I, 517).

RACHEL.

Or I to stay in his house, to give entertainment to this
knight or t'other coxcomb that comes to cheer him up with
eating of his cheer, when we must fetch 'em sweetmeats,
and they must tell us, "Ladies, your lips are sweeter,"
and then fall into courtship, one in a set speech taken out   60
of old Breton's works, another with verses out of *The
Academy of Compliments*, or some or other of the new poetical
pamphleteers, ambitious only to spoil paper and publish
their names in print. And then to be kiss'd, and sometimes
slaver'd. Fagh!   65

MERIEL.

'Tis not to be endur'd. We must out of the house. We cannot
live but by laughing, and that aloud, and nobody sad
within hearing.

VINCENT.

We are for any adventure with you, ladies. Shall we project
a journey for you? Your father has trusted you, and will   70
think you safe in our company; and we would fain be abroad
upon some progress with you. Shall we make a fling to
London, and see how the spring appears there in the
Spring Garden; and in Hyde Park, to see the races, horse

---

61. *Breton*] Nicholas Breton (1545–1626), author of over twenty-seven
prose tracts between 1580 and 1626 (N. E. Monroe, *Nicholas Breton as a
Pamphleteer*, [Philadelphia, 1929]). Brome is probably referring to *The
Arbor of Amorous Devises. Wherein, young Gentlemen may reade many plesent
fancies, and fine devises: And thereon, mediate divers sweete Conceites, to court the love
of faire Ladies and Gentlewomen*, edn. 1597.

61–62. *The Academy of Compliments*] or *Philomusus*, entered in the Stationers'
Register November 7, 1638: "Wherein Ladyes Gentlewomen, Schollers,
and Strangers may accomodate their Courtly Practice with most Curious
Ceremonies, Complementall, Amorous, High expressions, and formes of
speaking, or writing."

74. *Spring Garden*] eminent pleasure resort situated at the southeast corner
of what is now Trafalgar Square, a garden house and surrounding gardens
first erected as a retreat for royalty but later opened to the public. It is
mentioned along with Hyde Park and New Exchange in Phillips as
"esteemed the fittest Schools of Ceremony and Complement; where the
most select, as also the newest Fashions are alwayes in request" (sig. A3ᵛ).

74. *Hyde Park*] consisting of 360 acres contiguous to Kensington Gardens,
it was made into a public place in 1637 and was used for horse-racing until
1652 when the Commonwealth government sold it into private hands. It
resumed its reputation as a favorite rendezvous of fashion at the Restoration
in 1660

and foot; to hear the jockeys crack; and see the Adamites   75
run naked afore the ladies?

RACHEL.

We have seen all already there, as well as they, last year.

HILLIARD.

But there ha' been new plays since.

RACHEL.

No, no, we are not for London.

HILLIARD.

What think you of a journey to the Bath then?   80

RACHEL.

Worse than t'other way. I love not to carry my health
where others drop their diseases. Theres no sport i' that.

VINCENT.

Will you up to the hill top of sports, then, and merriments,
Dover's Olympics or the Cotswold Games.

MERIEL.

No, that will be too public for our recreation. We would   85
have it more within ourselves.

HILLIARD.

Think of some course yourselves then. We are for you upon
any way, as far as horse and money can carry us.

---

75. *crack*] boast.

75–76. *Adamites run naked*] originally a religious sect which adhered to
nakeness in imitation of Adam; here the naked runners in foot races, as
described by Phillipp Knyder in his seventeenth-century manuscript: "You
shal have in winters day, yᵉ earth crusted over with Ice, two Antagonists
starke naked runn a foote-race for 2. or 3. miles, with many hundred spec-
tators, & yᵉ betts very smale" (*The Historie of Darbyshire*, MS. Ashmole 788,
f. 197a; see also Joseph Strutt, *Sports and Pastimes*, edn. 1865, p. 66).

80. *Bath*] called by the Saxons "The City of sickly folke" described by
Camden in his account of Somersetshire: "three springs of hote water,"
which, "are very medicinable and of great vertue to cure bodies ouer-
charged and benummed . . . with corrupt humors" (p. 233).

84. *Dover's . . . Games*] For some years the Tuesday after Whitsunday
was associated with "Captain" Robert Dover's famous "Cotswold Games".
An attorney of Barton-on-the-heath in Warwickshire, he was celebrated in a
volume, *Annalia Dubrensia* (edn. 1636), as the restorer of the ancient Cotswold
Games of Elizabethan origin. The program of sports and pastimes consisted
of both athletic exercises, such as leaping, throwing the bar, running at
quintain, and field sports, such as coursing with greyhounds. An assembled
ring of country "gentiles" watched the sturdy shepherds contend for
mastery (so D. H. Madden, *The Diary of Master William Silence* [London,
1897], p. 171; *Sh. Eng.* II, 452).

VINCENT.

Ay, and if those means fail us, as far as our legs can bear, or
our hands can help us.   90

RACHEL.

And we will put you to't. —(*Aside.*)   Come aside, Meriel.

VINCENT.

Some jeer, perhaps, to put upon us.

HILLIARD.

What think you of a pilgrimage to St. Winifred's Well?

VINCENT.

Or a journey to the wise woman at Nantwich, to ask if we
be fit husbands for 'em?   95

HILLIARD.

They are not scrupulous in that, we having had their
growing loves up from our childhoods, and the old squire's
good will before all men.

RACHEL, MERIEL.

Ha, ha, ha—

VINCENT.

What's the conceit, I marvel?   100

RACHEL, MERIEL.

Ha, ha, ha, ha—

HILLIARD.

Some merry one, it seems.

RACHEL.

And then, sirrah Meriel— Hark again— Ha, ha, ha—

VINCENT.

How they are taken with it!

MERIEL.

Ha, ha, ha— Hark again, Rachel.   105

89. fail] *Q1* (faile); failes *Q2-3*.

---

93. *St. Winifred's Well*] a fountain and chapel, situated in the little town
of Haly-well, Flintshire, frequented by pilgrims in commemoration of the
"Christian Virgin Winefride, ravished there perforce and beheaded by the
tyrane as also for the mosse there growing of a most sweet and pleasant
smell" (Camden, p. 680).

94. *Nantwich*] "A town in Cheshire, on the Weaver, 17 m. S. E. of
Chester" (Sugden).

103. *sirrah*] sometimes applied to women as well as men; cf. Dekker's
The Honest Whore, Part I, (edn. 1604, sig. D2ᵛ): "Sirra Bellafronta."

HILLIARD.

Some wonderful nothing, sure. They will laugh as much to
see a swallow fly with a white feather imp'd in her tail.

VINCENT.

They were born laughing, I think.

RACHEL, MERIEL.

Ha, ha, ha—

VINCENT.

If it be not some trick upon us, which they'll discover in 110
some monstrous shape, they cozen me. —Now, ladies, is your
project ripe? Possess us with the knowledge of it.

RACHEL.

It is more precious than- to be imparted upon a slight
demand.

HILLIARD.

Pray, let us hear it. You know we are your trusty servants. 115

VINCENT.

And have kept all your counsels ever since we have been
infant playfellows.

RACHEL.

Yes, you have played at all kinds of small game with us,
but this is to the purpose. Ha, ha, ha—

HILLIARD.

It seems so by your laughing.   120

RACHEL.

And asks a stronger tongue-tie than tearing of books,
burning of samplers, making dirt pies, or piss and paddle in't.

VINCENT.

You know how, and what we have vow'd: to wait upon you
any way, any how, and any whither.

MERIEL.

And you will stand to't?   125

HILLIARD.

Ay, and go to't with you, wherever it be.

MERIEL.

Pray tell't 'em, sister Rachel.

---

107. *imp'd*] a term used in falconry in which feathers were engrafted in
the wing of a bird to make good any deficiencies and thereby restore or
improve the power of flight (Onions).

112. *Possess us*] inform us.

RACHEL.

    Why, gentlemen— Ha, ha— Thus it is— Tell it you, Meriel.

VINCENT.

    Oh, is that all?

MERIEL.

    You are the elder. Pray tell it you.   130

RACHEL.

    You are the younger. I command you tell it. Come, out with it; they long to have it.

HILLIARD.

    When?

VINCENT.

    When?

MERIEL.

    In troth you must tell it, sister; I cannot. Pray begin.   135

RACHEL.

    Then, gentlemen, stand your ground.

VINCENT.

    Some terrible business, sure!

RACHEL.

    You seem'd e'en now to admire the felicity of beggars—

MERIEL.

    And have engag'd yourselves to join with us in any course.

RACHEL.

    Will you now with us, and for our sakes turn beggars?   140

MERIEL.

    It is our resolution, and our injunction on you.

RACHEL.

    But for a time, and a short progress.

MERIEL.

    And for a spring-trick of youth, now, in the season.

VINCENT.

    Beggars! What rogues are these?

HILLIARD.

    A simple trial of our loves and service!   145

RACHEL.

    Are you resolv'd upon't? If not, God b'w'y'. We are resolv'd to take our course.

---

142. *progress*] journey.
146. *b'w'y'*] be with you.

MERIEL.

Let yours be to keep counsel.

VINCENT.

Stay, stay. Beggars! Are we not so already?
Do we not beg your loves, and your enjoyings?   150
Do we not beg to be receiv'd your servants?
To kiss your hands, or (if you will vouchsafe)
Your lips, or your embraces?

HILLIARD.   We now beg,
That we may fetch the rings and priest to marry us.
Wherein are we no beggars?   155

RACHEL.

That will not serve. Your time's not come for that yet.
You shall beg victuals first.

VINCENT.

Oh, I conceive your begging progress is to ramble out this
summer among your father's tenants; and 'tis in request
among gentlemen's daughters to devour their cheesecakes, 160
apple pies, cream and custards, flapjacks, and pan-
puddings.

MERIEL.

Not so, not so—

HILLIARD.

Why so we may be a kind of civil beggars.

RACHEL.

I mean stark, errant, downright beggars, ay,   165
Without equivocation; statute beggars.

MERIEL.

Couchant and passant, guardant, rampant beggars.

154. priest] *Q1;* Priests *Q2–3.*   166. equivocation] *Q1;* equivoca-
161. cream and custards] *Q2–3;*   tions *Q2–3.*
Cream Custards *Q1.*

---

165. *stark*] a pun: (1) thorough, (2) naked.
165. *errant*] a pun: (1) wandering, (2) wicked.
166. *statute beggars*] beggars defined by Statute 39 Eliz., c. 4 (1597–1598),
outlawing begging and severely punishing beggars by beatings, imprison-
ment, banishment, confinement in the galleys, or death as the case may be.
The proclamation was renewed September 17, 1630.
167. *Couchant*] lurking; in heraldry, lying down.
167. *passant*] fugitive; in heraldry, walking.

VINCENT.

    Current and vagrant—

HILLIARD.   Stockant, whippant beggars!

VINCENT.

    Must you and we be such? Would you so have it?

RACHEL.

    Such as we saw so merry, and you concluded   170
    Were th'only happy people in a nation.

MERIEL.

    The only free men of a commonwealth;
    Free above scot-free; that observe no law,
    Obey no governor, use no religion,
    But what they draw from their own ancient custom,   175
    Or constitute themselves, yet are no rebels.

RACHEL.

    Such as of all men's meat and all men's money
    Take a free part; and, wheresoe'er they travel,
    Have all things gratis to their hands provided.

VINCENT.

    Coarse fare most times.

RACHEL.   Their stomach makes it good;   180
    And feasts on that, which others scorn for food.

MERIEL.

    The antidote, content, is only theirs.
    And, unto that, such full delights are known,
    That they conceive the kingdom is their own.

VINCENT.

    'Fore Heaven I think they are in earnest, for they were   185
    always mad.

HILLIARD.

    And we were madder than they, if we should lose 'em.

VINCENT.

    'Tis but a mad trick of youth (as they say) for the spring or
    a short progress; and mirth may be made out of it, knew we
    how to carry it.   190

---

    168. *Current*] pun: (1) in vogue, (2) genuine.
    168. *Stockant*] "frequently set in the stocks" (*OED*).
    168. *whippant*] another nonce word, meaning frequently whipped.

RACHEL.

    Pray, gentlemen, be sudden.   *[Sound of]* cuckoo.

    Hark, you hear the cuckoo.

HILLIARD.

    We are most resolutely for you in your course.

VINCENT.

    But the vexation is how to set it on foot.

RACHEL.

    We have projected it. Now if you be perfect and constant 195
    lovers and friends, search you the means. —We have
    puzzl'd 'em.

MERIEL.

    I am glad on't. Let 'em pump.

VINCENT.

    Troth a small stock will serve to set up withal. This
    doublet sold off o' my back might serve to furnish a camp 200
    royal of us.

HILLIARD.

    But how to enter or arrange ourselves into the crew will
    be the difficulty. If we light raw and tame amongst 'em
    (like cage birds among a flight of wild ones) we shall never
    pick up a living, but have our brains peck'd out.   205

VINCENT.

    We want instruction dearly.

Enter Springlove.

HILLIARD.

    Oh, here comes Springlove. His great benefactorship among
    the beggars might prefer us with authority into a ragged
    regiment presently. Shall I put it to him?

RACHEL.

    Take heed what you do. His greatness with my father will 210
    betray us.

---

191. S.D. *cuckoo*] In Sussex, April 14 is called "first cuckoo day" (see
M. Aislabie Denham's *A Collection of Proverbs* in *Percy Society* [1846], XX,
42).

200–201. *a camp royal*] a host.

VINCENT.

I will cut his throat then. —My noble Springlove, the
great commander of the maunders and king of canters, we
saw the gratitude of your loyal subjects in the large
tributary content they gave you in their revels.   215

SPRINGLOVE.

Did you, sir?

HILLIARD.

We have seen all with great delight and admiration.

SPRINGLOVE.

I have seen you, too, kind gentlemen and ladies, and
overheard you in your quaint design to new create yourselves out of the worldly blessings and spiritual graces   220
Heaven has bestow'd upon you, to be partakers and
coactors, too, in those vile courses, which you call delights,
ta'en by those despicable and abhorred creatures.

VINCENT.

Thou art a despiser, nay a blasphemer
Against the maker of those happy creatures,   225
Who, of all human, have priority
In their content, in which they are so blest
That they enjoy most in possessing least.
Who made 'em such, dost think? Or why so happy?

RACHEL [aside to Meriel].

He grows zealous in the cause; sure he'll beg indeed.   230

HILLIARD.

Art thou an hypocrite, then, all this while?
Only pretending charity, or using it
To get a name and praise unto thyself;
And not to cherish and increase those creatures
In their most happy way of living? Or   235

---

213. *maunders*] beggars.
213. *canters*] beggars; those who "speake a Language (proper only to
themselves) called *canting* . . . Invented, to th' intent that (albeit any Spies
should secretly steale into their companies to discover them) they might
freely utter their mindes one to another, yet avoide the danger . . . And
very aptly may *canting* take his derivation *a cantando*, from singing, because
. . . the language of *canting* is a k[i]nde of musicke, and he that in such
assemblies can cant best, is counted the best Musitian" (*Lanthorne*, sigs.
B4–B4ᵛ).

Dost thou bestow thine alms with a foul purpose
To stint their begging, and with loss to buy
And slave those free souls from their liberty?

MERIEL [*aside to* Rachel].

They are more zealous in the cause than we.

SPRINGLOVE.

But are you, ladies, at defiance, too,   240
With reputation and the dignity
Due to your father's house and you?

RACHEL.

Hold thy peace, good Springlove, and though you seem to
dislike this course and reprove us for it, do not betray us
in it; your throat's in question. I tell you for good will, good   245
Springlove.

MERIEL.

What wouldst thou have us do? Thou talk'st o'th' house.
'Tis a base melancholy house. Our father's sadness banishes
us out on't. And for the delight thou tak'st in beggars and
their brawls, thou canst not but think they live a better   250
life abroad than we do in this house.

SPRINGLOVE.

I have sounded your faith, and I am glad I find you all
right. And for your father's sadness, I'll tell you the cause
on't. I overheard it but this day in his private discourse
with his merry mate, Master Hearty. He has been told   255
by some wizard that you both were born to be beggars.

ALL.

How. How!

SPRINGLOVE.

For which he is so tormented in mind, that he cannot sleep
in peace nor look upon you but with heart's grief.

VINCENT.

This is most strange.   260

RACHEL.

Let him be griev'd then till we are beggars.
We have just reason to become so now;
And what we thought on but in jest before,
We'll do in earnest now.

243–249. Hold . . . out on't] *printed
as verse in Q1–3.*

SPRINGLOVE.

Oh, I applaud this resolution in you; would have persuaded 265
it; will be your servant in't. For, look ye, ladies: The
sentence of your fortune does not say that you shall beg
for need, hunger or cold necessity. If, therefore, you
expose yourselves on pleasure into it, you shall absolve
your destiny nevertheless, and cure your father's grief. 270
I am overjoy'd to think on't; and will assist you faithfully.

ALL.

A Springlove! A Springlove!

SPRINGLOVE.

I am prepar'd already for th'adventure,
And will with all conveniences furnish
And set you forth, give you your dimensions,   275
Rules and directions. I will be your guide,
Your guard, your convoy, your authority.
You do not know my power, my command
I'th' beggars' commonwealth.

VINCENT.

But how? But how, good Springlove?   280

SPRINGLOVE.

I'll confess all. In my minority
My master took me up a naked beggar,
Bred me at school, then took me to his service
(You know in what good fashion); and you may
Collect to memory for seven late summers,   285
Either by leave, pretending friends to see
At far remote parts of the land, or else
By stealth, I would absent myself from service
To follow my own pleasure, which was begging,
Led to't by nature. My indulgent master   290
(Yet ignorant of my course) on my submission
When cold and hunger forc'd me back at winter,
Receiv'd me still again till, two years since,

265–266. Oh . . . ladies] *printed as*   268. hunger] *Coxeter;* Hungry *Q 1–3.*
verse in Q 1–3.

272. *A Springlove*] lover of spring; "a" is often used before proper names
connotatively with reference to the qualities of the individual.
275. *dimensions*] "measures" and proper "rhythm" appropriate in this
case for canting (*OED*).

He being drawn by journey towards the north
Where I then quarter'd with a ragged crew,   295
On the highway, not dreaming of him there,
I did accost him with a "Good your Worship,
The gift one small penny to a cripple"
(For here I was with him); "and the good Lord   *Halts.*
To bless you, and restore it you in Heaven."   300

ALL.

Ha, ha, ha.

SPRINGLOVE.

My head was dirty clouted, and this leg
Swaddled with rags, the other naked, and   *springlove unrecognized*
My body clad like his upon the gibbet.   *by Oldrents –*
Yet he, with searching eyes through all my rags   305
And counterfeit postures, made discovery
Of his man, Springlove; chid me into tears
And a confession of my forespent life.
At last, upon condition that vagary
Should be the last, he gave me leave to run   310
That summer out. In autumn home came I
In my home clothes again and former duty.
My master not alone conserv'd my counsel,
But lays more weighty trust and charge upon me;
Such was his love to keep me a home-man,   315
That he conferr'd his steward's place upon me,
Which clogg'd me the last year from those delights
I would not lose again to be his lord.

ALL.

A Springlove! A Springlove!

SPRINGLOVE.

Pursue the course you are on then, as cheerfully   320
As the inviting season smiles upon you.
Think how you are necessitated to it,
To quit your father's sadness and his fears
Touching your fortune. Till you have been beggars,
The sword hangs over him. You cannot think   325

---

299. S.D. *Halts*] i.e., limps.
325. *sword*] i.e., of Damocles; see Whitney's *Choice of Emblems* (edn. 1586,
p. 102): "a naked sworde, . . . Above his head . . . Which when he sawe,
as one distracte with care, Hee had no joye in mirthe, nor daintie fare."

Upon an act of greater piety
Unto your father, than t'expose yourselves
Brave volunteers, unpress'd by common need
Into this meritorious warfare; whence
(After a few days, or short season spent)   330
You bring him a perpetual peace and joy
By expiating the prophecy that torments him.
T'were worth your time in painful, woeful steps,
With your lives' hazard in a pilgrimage
So to redeem a father. But you'll find   335
A progress of such pleasure (as I'll govern't)
That the most happy courts could never boast
In all their tramplings on the country's cost;
Whose envy we shall draw, when they shall read
We outbeg them, and for as little need.   340

ALL.
A Springlove! A Springlove!

SPRINGLOVE.
Follow me, gallants, then, as cheerfully

Birds singing.

As— (Hark!) we are summon'd forth.

ALL.   We follow thee.   *Exeunt.*

[II.ii]   *Enter* Randall, *a purse in his hand.*

RANDALL.
Well, go thy ways. If ever any just or charitable steward
was commended, sure thou shalt be at the last quarter-day.
Here's five and twenty pounds for this quarter's beggar-
charge. And (if he return not by the end of this quarter)

---

332. *expiating*] averting.
338. *tramplings*] travel on foot.
[II.ii]
1–18. *Well . . . kingdom*] cf. Launcelot Gobbo's soliloquy about the
struggles between the fiend and his conscience (*Merchant of Venice*, II.ii).
2. *last quarter-day*] here in figurative sense; there are four days "fixed by
custom as marking off the quarters of the year, on which tenancy of houses
usually begins and ends, and the payment of rent and other quarterly
charges fall due: Lady Day (March 25), Midsummer Day (June 24),
Michaelmas Day (September 29), and Christmas (December 25)" (*OED*).
In Randall's speech "the end of this quarter" (l. 4) would be June 24.

here's order to a friend to supply for the next. If I now   5
should venture for the commendation of an unjust steward,
and turn this money to mine own use! Ha! Dear devil tempt
me not. I'll do thee service in a greater matter. But to
rob the poor! (a poor trick). Every churchwarden can
do't. Now something whispers me, that my master for his   10
steward's love will supply the poor as I may handle the
matter. Then I rob the steward if I restore him not the
money at his return. Away temptation, leave me. I am frail
flesh; yet I will fight with thee. But say the steward
never return. Oh, but he will return. Perhaps he may not   15
return. Turn from me, Satan; strive not to clog my conscience. I would not have this weight upon't for all thy   *Launce (mv)*
kingdom.   *passage —*

Enter Hearty *singing, and* Oldrents.

HEARTY.

   Hey down, hey down a down, &c.
   Remember, sir, your convenant to be merry.   20

OLDRENTS.

   I strive, you see, to be so.
   Yet something pricks me within, methinks.

HEARTY.

   No further thought, I hope, of fortune's telltales.

OLDRENTS.

   I think not of 'em. Nor will I presage
   That when a disposition of sadness   25
   O'erclouds my spirits, I shall therefore hear
   Ill news, or shortly meet with some disaster.

HEARTY.

   Nay, when a man meets with bad tidings, why
   May not he then compel his mind to mirth,
   As well as puling stomachs are made strong   30
   By eating against appetite?

30. puling] *Q1;* pulling *Q2–3.*

---

9. *churchwarden*] alusion to the corruptness of parochial clergy; cf.
Brome's *The Queen and the Concubine*, II.ii (edn. 1659, sig. C2ᵛ), where the
third clown says: "I would the Churchwarden that should have mended
it [the bell] when he robb'd the poor, were hang'd in's place."

OLDRENTS.

    Forc'd mirth though is not good.

HEARTY.

    It relishes not, you'll say. No more does meat
    That is most savory to a long sick stomach,
    Until by strife and custom 'tis made good.   35

OLDRENTS.

    You argue well. But do you see yond fellow?

HEARTY.

    I never noted him so sad before.
    He neither sings nor whistles.

OLDRENTS.   Something troubles him.

    Can he force mirth out of himself, now, think you?

HEARTY.

    What speak you of a clod of earth, a hind   40
    But one degree above a beast, compar'd
    To th'aery spirit of a gentleman?

OLDRENTS.

    He looks as he came laden with ill news,
    To meet me on my way.

HEARTY.   'Tis very pretty.

    Suppose the ass be tir'd with sadness; will you disburden him 45
    To load yourself? Think of your covenant to be merry
    In spite of fortune and her riddlemakers.

OLDRENTS.

    Why, how now Randall! Sad? Where's Springlove?

HEARTY [*aside*].

    He's ever in his care. But that I know
    The old squire's virtue, I should think Springlove   50
    Were sure his bastard.

RANDALL.   Here's his money, sir.

    I pray that I be charg'd with it no longer.
    The devil and I have strain'd courtesy these two hours
    about it. I would not be corrupted with the trust of more
    than is mine own. Mr. Steward gave it me, sir, to order 55

---

    41. *one degree*] a survival of the medieval conception of a rigidly ordered universe, here man's supremacy over the beast. The theory of the four humors is likewise alluded to, comparing the melancholy humor with the lowest element, earth or "clod" (l. 40), and the "aery spirit" (l. 42) of man with the elements of air and fire.

it for the beggars. He has made me steward of the barn
and them, while he is gone (he says) a journey to survey
and measure lands abroad about the countries. Some
purchase, I think, for your worship.

OLDRENTS.

I know his measuring of land. He is gone his old way.   60
And let him go. Am not I merry, Hearty?

HEARTY.

Yes, but not hearty merry. There's a whim now.

OLDRENTS.

The poor's charge shall be mine. Keep you the money
For him.

RANDALL.   Mine is the greater charge then.

Knew you but my temptations and my care,   65
You would discharge me of it.

OLDRENTS.   Ha, ha, ha.

RANDALL.

I have not had it so many minutes as I have been in several
minds about it, and most of them dishonest.

OLDRENTS.

Go then, and give it to one of my daughters to keep for
Springlove.   70

RANDALL.

Oh, I thank your worship.   *Exit.*

OLDRENTS.   Alas, poor knave!
How hard a task it is to alter custom!

HEARTY.

And how easy for money to corrupt it.
What a pure treasurer would he make!

OLDRENTS.

All were not born for weighty offices.   75
Which makes me think of Springlove.
He might have ta'en his leave though.

HEARTY.

I hope he's run away with some large trust.
I never lik'd such demure, downlook'd fellows.

OLDRENTS.

You are deceiv'd in him.   80

---

79. *demure*] serious, reserved.

HEARTY.

If you be not, 'tis well. But this is from the covenant.

OLDRENTS.

Well, sir, I will be merry. I am resolv'd
To force my spirit only unto mirth.
Should I hear now my daughters were misled
Or run away, I would not send a sigh   85
To fetch 'em back.

HEARTY.   T'other old song for that.

SONG

There was an old fellow at Waltham Cross,
Who merrily sung when he liv'd by the loss.
He never was heard to sigh with "Hey-ho,"
But sent it out with a "Haigh trolly lo."   90
   He cheer'd up his heart when his goods went to wrack,
   With a "Heghm, boy, heghm," and a cup of old sack.

OLDRENTS.

Is that the way on't? Well, it shall be mine then.

Enter Randall.

RANDALL.

My mistresses are both abroad, sir.

OLDRENTS.

How? since when?   95

RANDALL.

On foot, sir, two hours since, with the two gentlemen
their lovers. Here's a letter they left with the butler. And
there's a mutt'ring in the house.

OLDRENTS.

I will not read, nor open it; but conceive
Within myself the worst that can befall them;   100
That they are lost and no more mine. What follows?
That I am happy; all my cares are flown.

87–92.] Music, with the title "A Catch within a Catch (for Three Voices)"
by John Hilton, is printed in *Catch that Catch Can* (edn. 1652), p. 31.

87. *Waltham Cross*] "The Cross [was] erected there for the funerall
pompe of Queen Aeleonor wife to King Edward the First, whereof also it
[the town] tooke name" (Camden, p. 437).

The counsel I anticipated from
My friend shall serve to set my rest upon
(Without all further helps). To jovial mirth,   105
Which I will force out of my spleen so freely,
That grief shall lose her name where I have being;
And sadness, from my furthest foot of land
While I have life, be banish'd.

HEARTY.   What's the whim now?

OLDRENTS.

My tenants shall sit rent-free for this twelvemonth;   110
And all my servants have their wages doubled;
And so shall be my charge in housekeeping.
I hope my friends will find and put me to't.

HEARTY.

For them I'll be your undertaker, sir.
But this is overdone. I do not like it.   115

OLDRENTS.

And for thy news, the money that thou hast
Is now thine own. I'll make it good to Springlove.
Be sad with it and leave me. For I tell thee,
I'll purge my house of stupid melancholy.

RANDALL.

I'll be as merry as the charge that's under me.   120

A confused noise within of laughing and singing, and one crying out.

The beggars, sir. Do'ee hear 'em in the barn?

OLDRENTS.

I'll double their allowance too, that they may
Double their numbers, and increase their noise;
These bear not sound enough; and one (methought)
Cried out among 'em.   125

RANDALL.

By a most natural cause. For there's a doxy
Has been in labor, sir. And 'tis their custom,
With songs and shouts to drown the woman's cries,
A ceremony which they use, not for

---

104. *set . . . upon*] term in game of primero; to venture one's final stake
or reserve.

126. *doxy*] strumpet; more specifically explained in Harman: "These
Doxes be broken & spoyled of their maydenhead by the upright men, and
then they have their name of doxes, and not afore" (sig. F1ᵛ).

Devotion, but to keep off notice of   130
The work they have in hand. Now she is in
The straw, it seems; and they are quiet.

HEARTY.

The straw! That's very proper there. That's Randall's whim.

OLDRENTS.

We will have such a lying in, and such
A christ'ning, such upsitting and gossiping!   135
I mean to send forty miles' circuit at the least
To draw in all the beggars can be found,
And such devices we will have for jollity
As fame shall boast to all posterity.
Am I not merry, Hearty? hearty merry?   140

HEARTY.

Would you were else. I fear this overdoing,

OLDRENTS.

I'll do't for expiation of a crime
That's charg'd upon my conscience till't be done,

HEARTY.

What's that? What says he?

OLDRENTS.

We will have such a festival month on't, Randall—   145

RANDALL.

Sir, you may spare the labor and the cost;
They'll never thank you for't. They'll not endure
A ceremony that is not their own,
Belonging either to the child or mother.
A month, sir? They'll not be detain'd so long   150
For your estate. Their work is done already:
The bratling's born; the doxy's in the strummel,
Laid by an autem mort of their own crew,
That serv'd for midwife; and the childbed woman
Eating of hasty pudding for her supper,   155

131–132. *in/ The straw*] i.e., in childbed or lying in.
135. *gossiping*] a christening-feast.
152. *bratling*] little brat or infant.
152. *strummel*] canting term for straw.
153. *autem mort*] See "The Persons of the Play," l. 20, note.
155. *hasty pudding*] pun: pudding (1) made of flour stirred in boiling
water or milk, (2) prepared in haste.

And the child, part of it for pap,
I warrant you, by this time; then to sleep,
So to rise early to regain the strength
By travel, which she lost by travail.

HEARTY.
There's Randall again.

OLDRENTS.   Can this be?   160

RANDALL.
She'll have the bantling at her back tomorrow
That was today in her belly, and march a footback
With it.

HEARTY.   Art there again, old Randall?

RANDALL.
And for their gossiping (now you are so nigh)
If you'll look in, I doubt not, but you'll find 'em   165
At their high feast already.

HEARTY.   Pray let's see 'em, sir.

Randall *opens the scene. The* Beggars *discovered at their feast. After they have scrambled awhile at their victuals, this song.*

> *Here, safe in our skipper, let's cly off our peck,*
> *And bowse in defiance o'th' harman-beck.*
> *Here's pannum and lap, and good poplars of yarrum,*
> *To fill up the crib, and to comfort the quarron.*   170

---

161. *bantling*] bastard.
162. *a footback*] on foot (cf. horseback).
166.1. *opens the scene*] opens curtains to inner stage.
167–182.] Similar canting songs, with translations, are printed in *Eng. Vil.*, sigs. O1ᵛ ff.
167. *skipper*] barn (*Eng. Vil.*, sig. N4); "possibly derived from Cornish *scriber* or W[elsh] *ysgubor*" (*OED*).
167. *cly*] seize or take (Harman, sig. G4).
167. *peck*] meat, grub (*Eng. Vil.*, sig. N4ᵛ).
168. *bowse*] to swill, drink to excess for enjoyment (*Eng. Vil.*, sig. N3ᵛ).
168. *harman-beck*] constable or beadle (*Eng. Vil.*, sig. N4; Harman, sig. G4).
169. *pannum*] bread, coined from Latin *Panis* (Harman, sig. G4).
169. *lap*] buttermilk, or whey (*Eng. Vil.*, sig. N3ᵛ; Harman, sig. G4).
169. *poplars of yarrum*] milk pottage (*Eng. Vil.*, sig. N4ᵛ); "Poppelars" [porrage], "yeram" [mylke] (Harman, sig. G4).
170. *crib*] food supply.
170. *quarron*] body (*Eng. Vil.*, sig. N4ᵛ; Harman, sig. G2ᵛ).

Now bowse a round health to the go-well and come-well
Of Cisley Bumtrinket that lies in the strummel.
Now bowse a round health to the go-well and come-well
Of Cisley Bumtrinket that lies in the strummel.

Here's ruff-peck and casson, and all of the best,   175
And scraps of the dainties of gentry cove's feast.
Here's grunter and bleater, with Tib of the butt'ry,
And Margery Prater, all dress'd without slutt'ry.
For all this bene cribbing and peck let us then
Bowse a health to the gentry cove of the ken.   180
Now bowse a round health to the go-well and come-well
Of Cisley Bumtrinket that lies in the strummel.

OLDRENTS.

Good heaven, how merry they are.

HEARTY.   Be not you sad at that.

OLDRENTS.

Sad, Hearty, no, unless it be with envy
At their full happiness. What is an estate   185
Of wealth and power, balanc'd with their freedom,
But a mere load of outward compliment,
When they enjoy the fruits of rich content?
Our dross but weighs us down into despair,
While their sublimed spirits dance i'th' air.   190

HEARTY.

I ha' not so much wealth to weigh me down,
Nor so little (I thank Chance) as to dance naked.

---

171. *go-well*] "prosperous journey outward" (*OED*); hence nonce use of "come and go."

171. *come-well*] birth; i.e., to come into this world.

172. *Cisley Bumtrinket*] common appellation for female servant; as in Dekker's *Shoemakers' Holiday* (edn. 1600, sig. C3) and "Sisley" in Jonson's *Gypsies Metamorphosed* (edn. 1640, sig. d14).

175. *ruff-peck*] bacon (Harman, sig. G4).

175. *casson*] cheese (*Eng. Vil.*, sig. N2ᵛ).

176. *gentry cove*] a gentleman (*Eng. Vil.*, sig. N4).

177. *grunter*] pig; namely, "a grunting chete" (Harman, sig. G4).

177. *bleater*] calf or sheep; a "bleting chete" (Harman, sig. G4).

177. *Tib of the butt'ry*] a fat goose (*Eng. Vil.*, sigs. O3ᵛ–O4).

178. *Margery Prater*] hen (*Eng. Vil.*, sig. N4; Harman, sig. G4).

179. *bene cribbing*] good food, provender, provisions.

180. *ken*] house (Harman, sig. G4).

OLDRENTS.

> True, my friend Hearty, thou having less than I
> (Of which I boast not), art the merrier man;
> But they exceed thee in that way so far   195
> That should I know my children now were beggars
> (Which yet I will not read), I must conclude
> They were not lost, nor I to be aggriev'd.

HEARTY.

> If this be madness, 'tis a merry fit.

> *Enter* Patrico. *Many of the* Beggars *look out.*

PATRICO.

> Tour out with your glaziers; I swear by the ruffin   200
> That we are assaulted by a queer cuffin.

RANDALL.

> Hold! What d'ee mean, my friends? This is our master,
> The master of your feast and feasting house.

PATRICO.

> Is this the gentry cove?

ALL THE BEGGARS.

> Lord bless his worship. His good worship. Bless his worship. 205
> > *Exeunt* Beggars, *manet* Patrico.

PATRICO.

> Now, bounteous sir, before you go,
> Hear me, the beggar patrico;
> Or priest, if you do rather choose
> That we no word of canting use.
> Long may you live, and may your store   210
> Never decay nor balk the poor;
> And as you more in years do grow,
> May treasure to your coffers flow;
> And may your care no more thereon
> Be set, than ours are, that have none.   215
> But as your riches do increase,
> So may your heart's content and peace.

---

200. *Tour out*] look out (*Eng. Vil.*, sigs. O1–O2; Harman, sig. G4ᵛ).
200. *glaziers*] eyes (*Eng. Vil.*, sig. N4; Harman, sig. G2ᵛ).
200. *ruffin*] devil (*Eng. Vil.*, sig. N4ᵛ).
201. *queer cuffin*] justice of peace (Harman, sig. G4).
209. *canting*] See II.i.213, note.   211. *balk*] disappoint (*OED*).

And after many, many years,
When the poor have quit their fears
Of losing you, and that with Heaven   220
And all the world you have made even,
Then may your blest posterity,
Age after age successively
Until the world shall be untwin'd,
Inherit your estate and mind.   225
So shall the poor to the last day
For you, in your succession, pray.

HEARTY.

'Tis a good vote, Sir Patrico, but you are too grave. Let
us hear and see something of your merry grigs, that can
sing, play gambols, and do feats.   230

PATRICO.

Sir, I can lay my function by
And talk as wild and wantonly
As Tom or Tib, or Jack, or Jill,
When they at bowsing ken do swill.
Will you, therefore, deign to hear   235
My autem mort, with throat as clear
As was Dame Annis's of the name;
How sweet in song her notes she'll frame,
That when she chides, as loud is yawning
As Chanticleer wak'd by the dawning.   240

HEARTY.

Yes, pray let's hear her. What is she, your wife?

PATRICO.

Yes, sir. We of our ministry,
As well as those o'th' presbytery,
Take wives and defy dignity.   *Exit.*

HEARTY.

A learned clerk in verity!   245

---

229. *merry grigs*] "extravagantly lively persons . . . full of frolic and jest"
(*OED*).

234. *bowsing ken*] ale house (Harman, sig. G4; *Eng. Vil.*, sig. N3ᵛ).

237. *Dame Annis's*] a well, "somewhat North from Holywell . . . curbed
square with stone, and is called Dame Annis the cleere" (John Stow,
A Survey of London, edn. 1633, Chap. III, p. 11).

243. *presbytery*] Scottish Presbyterians, whose national covenant denounced
all ecclesiastical measures inconsistent with the principles of the reformation.

Enter Patrico *with his old wife, with a wooden bowl of drink. She is drunk.*

PATRICO.

By Salmon, I think my mort is in drink.
I find by her stink, and the pretty, pretty pink
Of her neyes, that half wink,
That the tippling feast, with the doxy in the neast,
Hath turn'd her brain, to a merry, merry vein.   250

AUTEM MORT.

Go fiddle, Patrico, and let me sing. First set me down
here on both my prats. Gently, gently, for cracking of my
wind, now I must use it. Hem, hem.

She sings.

This is bene bowse; this is bene bowse;
    Too little is my skew.   255
I bowse no lage, but a whole gage
    Of this I'll bowse to you.
This bowse is better than rum bowse;
    It sets the gan a-giggling.
The autem mort finds better sport   260
    In bowsing than in niggling.

This is bene bowse, &c.

She tosses off her bowl, falls back, and is carried out.

PATRICO.

So, so; your part is done.   *Exit with her.*

HEARTY.

How find you, sir, yourself?

OLDRENTS.

Wondrous merry, my good Hearty.   265

---

246. *By Salmon*] i.e., "By Solomon", meaning "by the masse"; according
to S. Rowland's *Martin Markall, Beadle of Bridewell* (edn. 1610, sig. E4), to
swear by his Solomon is a rogue's inviolable oath.
248. *neyes*] eyes.   252. *prats*] buttocks (*Eng. Vil.*, sig. N4).
254–262.] The same song is printed in *The English Rogue, the Second Part*,
edn. 1668, pp. 131–132.
254. *bene bowse*] good drinking.   255. *skew*] cup (*Eng. Vil.*, sig. N4).
256. *lage*] water (*Eng. Vil.*, sig. N4; Harman, sig. G4).
256. *gage*] quart-pot (Harman, sig. G4); or "Dwarf-pot" (*Eng. Vil.*,
sig. N4).
258. *rum bowse*] wine (*Eng. Vil.*, sig. N4ᵛ; Harman, sig. G4).
259. *gan*] mouth (*Eng. Vil.*, Sig. N4; Harman, sig. G2ᵛ).
261. *niggling*] copulating.

Enter Patrico.

PATRICO.

    I wish we had in all our store
    Something that could please you more.
    The old or autem mort's asleep;
    But before the young ones creep
    Into the straw, sir, if you are   270
    (As gallants sometimes love coarse fare,
    So it be fresh and wholesome ware)
    Dispos'd to doxy, or a dell,
    That never yet with man did mell;
    Of whom no upright-man is taster,   275
    I'll present her to you, master.

OLDRENTS.

    Away! You would be punish'd. Oh!

HEARTY.

    How is it with you, sir?

OLDRENTS.

    A sudden qualm overchills my stomach, but 'twill away.

Enter Dancers.

PATRICO.

    See in their rags, then, dancing for your sports,   280
    Our clapperdudgeons and their walking morts.

---

    273. *dell*] "A Dell is a yonge wench, able for generation, and not yet known or broken by the upright man" (Harman, sig. G1).

    274. *mell*] copulate.

    275. *upright-man*] second in degree of the order of beggars. Some are servingmen, artificers, and laboring men trained in husbandry who chose not to get their living by "the sweat of their face" (Harman, sig. B2^v). For further details see *Belman*, sigs. C4–C4^v.

    281. *clapperdudgeons*] beggars; also called "palliards," best described by Harman, sigs. C3^v–C4. Collier suggests in his notes that the appellation originated with the beggar's habit of knocking the clapdish he carried with a dudgeon.

    281. *walking morts*] According to Dekker's *Belman* (sig. E1), "The Walking mort is of more antiquitie than a Doxie, and therefore of more knaverie: they both are unmarried, but the Doxie professes her selfe to be a maide (if it come to examination) and the Walking mort says, she is a widdow, whose husband died eyther in the Portugall voyage, was slaine in Ireland, or the Low Countries, or came to his end by some other misfortune, leaving her so many small infants on her hand in debt." See also Harman, sig. F1^v.

Dance.

You have done well. Now let each tripper
Make a retreat into the skipper,
And couch a hogshead, till the darkman's pass'd;
Then all with bag and baggage bing awast.   *Exeunt* Beggars.   285

RANDALL.

I told you, sir, they would be gone tomorrow.
I understand their canting.

OLDRENTS.

Take that amongst you.   *Gives money.*

PATRICO.

May rich plenty so you bless
Though you still give, you ne'er have less.   *Exit.*   290

HEARTY.

And as your walks may lead this way,
Pray strike in here another day.
So you may go, Sir Patrico—
How think you, sir? Or what? Or why do you think at all,
unless on sack and supper time? Do you fall back? Do you   295
not know the danger of relapses?

OLDRENTS.

Good Hearty, thou mistak'st me. I was thinking upon this
Patrico. And that he has more soul than a born beggar in
him.

HEARTY.

Rogue enough though, to offer us his what-d'ee-call'ts?   300
his doxies. Heart and a cup of sack, do we look like old
beggar-nigglers?

OLDRENTS.

Pray forbear that language.

HEARTY.

Will you then talk of sack that can drown sighing? Will
you in to supper, and take me there your guest? Or must   305
I creep into the barn among your welcome ones?

---

284. *couch a hogshead*] "To ly downe and slepe" (Harman, sig. G4ᵛ).
284. *darkman*] night (*Eng. Vil.*, sig. N4; Harman, sig. G4).
285. *bing awast*] "go you hence" (Harman, sig. G4ᵛ; *Eng. Vil.*, sig. N3ᵛ)
302. *beggar-nigglers*] lascivious persons; "niggling" in cant language
means "companying with a woman" (*Eng. Vil.*, sig. N4); cf. above, l. 261,
note.

OLDRENTS.

You have rebuk'd me timely, and most friendly.   *Exit.*

HEARTY.

Would all were well with him.   *Exit.*

RANDALL.   It is with me,

For now these pounds are (as I feel them swag)

Light at my heart, though heavy in the bag.   *Exit.* 310

[III.i]   [*Enter*] Vincent *and* Hilliard *in their rags.*

VINCENT.

Is this the life that we admir'd in others, with envy at
their happiness?

HILLIARD.

Pray let us make virtuous use of it, and repent us of that
deadly sin (before a greater punishment than famine and
lice fall upon us) by steering our course homeward. Before   5
I'll endure such another night—

VINCENT.

What? What wouldst thou do? I would thy mistress
heard thee.

HILLIARD.

I hope she does not, for I know there is no altering our
course before they make the first motion.   10

VINCENT.

Is't possible we should be weary already? And before their
softer constitutions of flesh and blood?

HILLIARD.

They are the stronger in will, it seems.

Enter Springlove.

SPRINGLOVE.

How now, comrades! Repining already at your fulness of
liberty? Do you complain of ease?   15

VINCENT.

Ease, call'st thou it? Didst thou sleep tonight?

SPRINGLOVE.

Not so well these eighteen months, I swear, since my last
walks.

HILLIARD.

Lightning and tempest is out of thy litany. Could not the
thunder wake thee?   20

SPRINGLOVE.

Ha, ha, ha.

VINCENT.

Nor the noise of the crew in the quarter by us?

HILLIARD.

Nor the hogs in the hovel that cried till they drown'd the
noise of the wind? If I could but once ha' dreamt in all my
former nights that such an affliction could have been found   25
among beggars, sure I should never have travel'd to the
proof on't.

VINCENT.

We look'd upon them in their jollity, and cast no further.

HILLIARD.

Nor did that only draw us forth (by your favor, Vince), but
our obedience to our loves, which we must suffer till they   30
cry home again. Are they not weary yet, as much as we,
dost think, Springlove?

SPRINGLOVE.

They have more moral understanding than so. They know
(and so may you) this is your birthnight into a new world. *we come crying*
And we all know (or have been told) that all come crying   35 *hither –*
into the world, when the whole world of pleasures is before
us. The world itself had ne'er been glorious, had it not
first been a confused chaos.

VINCENT.

Well, never did knight-errants in all adventures merit more
of their ladies than we beggar-errants, or errant beggars,   40
do in ours.

SPRINGLOVE.

The greater will be your reward. Think upon that. And show
no manner of distate to turn their hearts from you. Y'are
undone then.

HILLIARD.

Are they ready to appear out of their privy lodgings in   45
the pig's palace of pleasure? Are they coming forth?

---

46. *pig's palace of pleasure*] an allusion to Painter's *The Palace of Pleasure*
(edn. 1566).

SPRINGLOVE.

I left 'em almost ready, sitting on their pads of straw helping to dress each other's heads (the one's eye is the t'other's looking glass) with the prettiest coil they keep to fit their fancies in the most graceful way of wearing their new dressings, that you would admire.   50

VINCENT.

I hope we are as gracefully set out. Are we not?

SPRINGLOVE.

Indifferent well. But will you fall to practice? Let me hear how you can maund when you meet with passengers.

HILLIARD.

We do not look like men, I hope, too good to learn.   55

SPRINGLOVE.

Suppose some persons of worth or wealth passing by now. Note me. "Good your good worship, your charity to the poor, that will duly and truly pray for you day and night—"

VINCENT.

"Away you idle rogue; you would be set to work and whipp'd—"   60

SPRINGLOVE.

"That is lame and sick, hungry and comfortless—"

VINCENT.

"If you were well serv'd—"

SPRINGLOVE.

"And even to bless you and reward you for it—"

HILLIARD.

Prithee, hold thy peace (here be doleful notes indeed) and leave us to our own genius. If we must beg, let's let it go as it   65 comes, by inspiration. I love not your set form of begging.

SPRINGLOVE.

Let me instruct ye though.

Enter Rachel *and* Meriel *in rags.*

---

49. *coil*] turmoil.
54. *maund*] beg.
59–60. *set . . . whipp'd*] another reference to the statute against beggars; see II.i.166, note.

RACHEL.

Have a care, good Meriel, what hearts or limbs soever we
have, and though never so feeble, let us set our best faces
on't, and laugh our last gasp out before we discover any   70
dislike or weariness to them. Let us bear it out till they
complain first, and beg to carry us home a-pick-pack.

MERIEL.

I am sorely surbated with hoofing already though, and so
crupper-cramp'd with our hard lodging, and so bumfiddled
with the straw, that—   75

RACHEL.

Think not on't. I am numb'd i'the bum and shoulders, too,
a little. And have found the difference between a hard
floor with a little straw, and a down bed with a quilt
upon't. But no words, nor a sour look, I prithee.

HILLIARD.

Oh, here they come now, Madam Fewclothes and my Lady   80
Bonnyrag.

VINCENT.

Peace, they see us.

RACHEL, MERIEL.

Ha, ha, ha.

VINCENT.

We are glad the object pleases ye.

RACHEL.

So does the subject.   85

Now you appear the glories of the spring,
Darlings of Phoebus and the summer's heirs.

HILLIARD.

How fairer than fair Flora's self appear
(To deck the spring) Diana's darlings dear!
Oh let us not Acteon-like be strook   90

---

79. nor] *Q1;* not *Q2–3.*

72. *a-pick-pack*] on the shoulder or back.
73. *surbated*] foot-sore.
74. *bumfiddled*] posterior pricked with straw.
90. *Acteon-like*] Ovid, *Met.* III.138–152. Acteon was turned into a stag
(l. 93) as punishment for spying upon Diana's nakedness.
90. *strook*] struck.

(With greedy eyes while we presume to look
On your half nakedness, since courteous rags
Cover the rest) into the shape of stags.

RACHEL, MERIEL.

Ha, ha, ha. We are glad you are so merry.

VINCENT.

Merry and lusty, too. This night will we lie together as   95
well as the proudest couple in the barn.

HILLIARD.

And so will we. I can hold out no longer.

RACHEL.

Does the straw stir up your flesh to't, gentlemen?

MERIEL.

Or does your provender prick you?

SPRINGLOVE.

What! do we come for this? Laugh and lie down   100
When your bellies are full. Remember, ladies,
You have not begg'd yet, to quit your destiny,
But have liv'd hitherto on my endeavors.
Who got your suppers, pray, last night, but I,
Of dainty trencher-fees, from a gentleman's house,   105
Such as the serving-men themselves, sometimes,
Would have been glad of? And this morning now,
What comfortable chippings and sweet buttermilk
Had you to breakfast?

RACHEL.   Oh, 'twas excellent!

I feel it good still, here.   110

95. will we lie] *Q1–2;* we will lye
Q3.

---

96. *barn*] cf. Harman (sig. A3^v), for a description of beggar revelry in
barns: "seven score persons of men, every of them having his woman . . .
the buriall was tourned to bousing and belly cheere, mourning to myrth,
fasting to feasting, prayer to pastyme, and pressing of paps and lamenting
to lecherye." The ocasion in this instance was the burial of "a man of much
worship in Kent" who died immediately after the decapitation of the Duke
of Buckingham, May 1521.

100. *Laugh . . . down*] see II.i.49–50, note.

102. *quit*] "To rid (oneself) of" (*OED*).

105. *trencher-fees*] scraps of food given in alms.

108. *chippings*] parings of the crust of a loaf.

MERIEL.

There was a brown crust amongst it that has made my
neck so white, methinks. Is it not, Rachel?

RACHEL.

Yes, you ga' me none on't.
You ever covet to have all the beauty.
'Tis the ambition of all younger sisters.   115

VINCENT.

They are pleas'd, and never like to be weary.

HILLIARD.

No more must we, if we'll be theirs.

SPRINGLOVE.

Peace. Here come passengers. Forget not your rules, and
quickly disperse yourselves, and fall to your calling—
                          [*Exeunt* Hilliard, Rachel, Meriel.]

Enter two Gentlemen.

1 GENTLEMAN.

Lead the horses down the hill. The heat of our speed is 120
over, for we have lost our journey.

2 GENTLEMAN.

Had they taken this way, we had overtaken 'em, or heard of
'em at least.

1 GENTLEMAN.

But some of our scouts will light on 'em, the whole country
being overspread with 'em.   125

2 GENTLEMAN.

There was never such an escape else.

VINCENT.

A search for us perhaps. Yet I know not them, nor they
me, I am sure. I might the better beg of 'em. But how to
begin, or set the worst leg forwards, would I were whipp'd
if I know now.   130

1 GENTLEMAN.

That a young gentlewoman of her breeding, and heir to
such an estate, should fly from so great a match and run
away with her uncle's clerk!

2 GENTLEMAN.

> The old justice will run mad upon't, I fear.

VINCENT.

> If I were to be hang'd now, I could not beg for my life. 135

SPRINGLOVE.

> Step forwards and beg handsomely. I'll set my goad i'
> your breech else.

VINCENT.

> What shall I say?

SPRINGLOVE.

> Have I not told you? Now begin.

VINCENT [*pushing* Springlove *forward*].

> After you, good Springlove. 140

SPRINGLOVE.

> Good, your good worships—

1 GENTLEMAN.

> Away you idle vagabond—

SPRINGLOVE.

> Your worship's charity to a poor critter welly starv'd.

VINCENT.

> That will duly and truly pray for ye.

2 GENTLEMAN.

> You counterfeit villains, hence. 145

SPRINGLOVE.

> Good masters' sweet worship, for the tender mercy of—

VINCENT.

> Duly and truly pray for you.

1 GENTLEMAN.

> You would be well whipp'd and set to work, if you were
> duly and truly serv'd.

VINCENT [*aside*].

> Did not I say so before? 150

SPRINGLOVE.

> Good worshipful masters' worship, to bestow your charity,
> and, to maintain your health and limbs—

VINCENT.

> Duly and truly pray for you.

---

143. *critter welly*] North Scotland dialect for "creature" and "well-nigh"
(Wright).

2 GENTLEMAN.

Begone, I say, you impudent, lusty young rascals.

1 GENTLEMAN.

I'll set you going else.   *Switch 'em.* 155

SPRINGLOVE.

Ah, the goodness of compassion to soften your hearts to the
poor.

VINCENT [*to* Springlove].

Oh, the devil; must not we beat 'em now? Steth—

SPRINGLOVE.

Nor show an angry look for all the skin of our backs. —Ah,
the sweetness of that mercy that gives to all, to move your 160
compassion to the hungry, when it shall seem good unto you,
and night and day to bless all that you have. Ah, ah—

2 GENTLEMAN.

Come back, sirrah. His patience and humility has wrought
upon me.

VINCENT.

Duly and—   165

2 GENTLEMAN.

Not you, sirrah. The t'other. —You look like a sturdy rogue.

SPRINGLOVE.

Lord bless you, Master's worship.

2 GENTLEMAN.

There's a halfpenny for you. Let him have no share with you.

VINCENT [*aside*].

I shall never thrive o' this trade.

1 GENTLEMAN.

They are of a fraternity, and will share, I warrant you.   170

SPRINGLOVE.

Never in our lives, truly. He never begg'd with me before.

1 GENTLEMAN.

But if hedges or hen roosts could speak, you might be found
sharers in pillage, I believe.

---

158. *Steth*] euphemistic abbreviation of "God's death."
170. *fraternity*] Dekker in *O Per Se O*, (edn. 1612, sigs. N2ᵛ–N3), writes
"Of their fraternities": "There is no lustie Roague, but hath many both
sworne Brothers, and the Morts his sworne Sisters: who vow themselves
body and soule to the Divell to performe these tenne Articles," i.e., rules of
conduct to which each begger is sworn.

SPRINGLOVE.

Never saw him before, bless you, good master, in all my
life. [*To* Vincent.] Beg for yourself. Your credit's gone 175
else. [*To* Gentlemen.] Good hea'en to bliss and prosper ye.

Exit.

2 GENTLEMAN.

Why dost thou follow us? Is it your office to be privy to
our talk?

VINCENT.

Sir, I beseech you hear me. —(S'life, what shall I say?)—
I am a stranger in these parts, and destitute of means and 180
apparel.

1 GENTLEMAN.

So methinks. And what o' that?

VINCENT.

Will you, therefore, be pleas'd, as you are worthy gentlemen,
and blest with plenty—

2 GENTLEMAN.

This is courtly! 185

VINCENT.

Out of your abundant store, towards my relief in extreme
necessity to furnish me with a small parcel of money,
five or six pieces, or ten, if you can presently spare it.

1, 2 GENTLEMEN.

Stand off. *Draw.*

VINCENT [*aside*].

I have spoil'd all, and know not how to beg otherwise. 190

1 GENTLEMAN.

Here's a new way of begging!

VINCENT [*aside*].

Quite run out of my instructions.

2 GENTLEMAN.

Some highway thief, o' my conscience, that forgets he is
weaponless.

VINCENT.

Only to make you merry, gentlemen, at my unskillfulness in 195
my new trade. I have been another man i' my days. So I
kiss your hands. *Exit.*

176. *bliss*] bless.
188. *pieces*] "gold coins, or *unites*, worth 22 shillings each in 1612" (*OED*).

1 GENTLEMAN.

With your heels, do you?

2 GENTLEMAN.

It had been good to have apprehended the rakeshame.
There is some mystery in his rags. But let him go.   200

Enter Oliver, *putting up his sword.*

OLIVER.

You found your legs in time. I had made you halt for
something else.

1 GENTLEMAN.

Master Oliver, well return'd; what's the matter, sir?

OLIVER.

Why, sir, a counterfeit lame rogue begg'd of me, but in
such language the high sheriff's son o'the shire could not 205
have spoke better, nor to have borrowed a greater sum. He
ask'd me if I could spare him ten or twenty pound. I
switch'd him; his cudgel was up. I drew, and into the
wood he 'scap'd me, as nimbly—but first he told me, I
should hear from him by a gentleman, to require satisfaction 210
of me.

2 GENTLEMAN.

We had such another begg'd of us. The court goes a-begging,
I think.

1 GENTLEMAN.

Dropp'd through the clouds, I think; more Lucifers, travel-
ing to hell, that beg by the way. Met you no news of your 215
kinswoman, Mistress Amie?

OLIVER.

No. What's the matter with her? Goes her marriage
forwards with young master Tallboy? I hasten'd my journey
from London to be at the wedding.

2 GENTLEMAN.

'Twas to ha' been yesterday morning; all things in readi- 220
ness prepar'd for it. But the bride, stol'n by your father's
clerk, is slipp'd away. We were in quest of 'em, and so are
twenty more, several ways.

205. shire] *Q1–2;* sire *Q3.*

---

199. *rakeshame*] term for an "ill-behaved, disorderly or dissolute fellow"
(*OED*).

OLIVER.

Such young wenches will have their own ways in their own
loves, what matches soever their guardians make for 'em. 225
And I hope my father will not follow the law so close to
hang his clerk for stealing his ward with her own consent.
It may breed such a grudge, may cause some clerks to hang
their masters, that have 'em o'the hip of injustice. Besides,
Martin (though he be his servant) is a gentleman. But, 230
indeed, the miserablest rascal! He will grudge her meat
when he has her.

1 GENTLEMAN.

Your father is exceedingly troubled at their escape. I wish
that you may qualify him with your reasons.

OLIVER.

But what says Tallboy to the matter, the bridegroom that 235
should ha' been?

2 GENTLEMAN.

Marry, he says little to the purpose, but cries outright.

OLIVER.

I like him well for that: he holds his humor. A miserable
wretch, too, though rich. I ha' known him cry when he has
lost but three shillings at mumchance. But, gentlemen, 240
keep on your way to comfort my father. I know some of his
man's private haunts about the country here, which I will
search immediately.

1 GENTLEMAN.

We will accompany you, if you please.

OLIVER.

No, by no means; that will be too public. 245

2 GENTLEMAN.

Do your pleasure. *Exeunt two* Gentlemen.

OLIVER.

My pleasure and all the search that I intend is, by hovering
here, to take a review of a brace of the handsomest beggar-
brachs that ever grac'd a ditch or a hedge-side. I pass'd by

246. S.D. *Exeunt*] *Reed; Exit 1.2.*
Q1–3.

---

234. *qualify*] appease.
240. *mumchance*] a dicing game similar to hazard, in which strict silence
is observed. (See *Sh. Eng.*, II, 470–471.)
248–249. *beggar-brachs*] term of contempt, from "brach," a bitch-hound.

'em in haste, but something so possesses me, that I must— 250
What the devil must I? A beggar? Why, beggars are flesh
and blood, and rags are no diseases. Their lice are no
French fleas. And there is much wholesomer flesh under
country dirt than city painting, and less danger in dirt and
rags, than in ceruse and satin. I durst not take a touch at 255
London, both for the present cost and fear of an after-
reckoning. But, Oliver, dost thou speak like a gentleman?
Fear price or pox, ha? Marry, do I, sir; nor can beggar-
sport be inexcusable in a young country gentleman short
of means for another respect, a principal one indeed, to 260
avoid the punishment or charge of bastardy. There's no
commuting with them, or keeping of children for them. The
poor whores, rather than part with their own or want
children at all, will steal other folks' to travel with and
move compassion. He feeds a beggar-wench well that 265
fills her belly with young bones. And these reasons considered, good master Oliver—s'lid, yonder they are at
peep. And now sitten down as waiting for my purpose.

Enter Vincent.

Heart, here's another delay. I must shift him. —Dost
hear, honest poor fellow? I prithee, go back presently, 270
and at the hill-foot (here's sixpence for thy pains) thou
shalt find a footman with a horse in his hand. Bid him
wait there. His master will come presently, say.

VINCENT.

Sir, I have a business of another nature to you. Which
(as I presume you are a gentleman of right noble spirit 275
and resolution) you will receive without offense, and in
that temper as most properly appertains to the most heroic
natures.

OLIVER.

Thy language makes me wonder at thy person. What's the
matter with thee? Quickly.   280

VINCENT.

You may be pleas'd to call to mind a late affront, which,
in your heat of passion, you gave a gentleman.

---

255. *ceruse*] "White lead, wheerewith women paint" (Cotgrave).
267–268. *at peep*] similar in construction to "at play"; both girls are
furtively peering over the hedge.

OLIVER.

What, such a one as thou art, was he?

VINCENT.

True, noble sir. Who could no less in honor than direct
me, his chosen friend, unto you with the length of his 285
sword, or to take the length of yours. The place, if you
please, the ground whereon you parted; the hour, seven the
next morning; or, if you like not these, in part, or all, to
make your own appointments.

OLIVER [aside].

The bravest method in beggars that ever was discovered! 290
I would be upon the bones of this rogue now but for crossing
my other design, which fires me. I must, therefore, be rid
of him on any terms. —Let his own appointments stand.
Tell him I'll meet him.

VINCENT.

You shall most nobly engage his life to serve you, sir.   295

OLIVER.

You'll be his second, will you?

VINCENT.

To do you further service, sir, I have undertaken it.

OLIVER.

I'll send a beadle shall undertake you both.

VINCENT.

Your mirth becomes the bravery of your mind and dauntless
spirit. So takes his leave, your servant, sir.   [Exit.] 300

OLIVER.

I think, as my friend said, the court goes a-begging indeed.
But I must not lose my beggar-wenches.

                    Enter Rachel and Meriel.

Oh, here they come. They are delicately skin'd and limb'd.
There, there, I saw above the ham as the wind blew. Now
they spy me.   305

RACHEL.

Sir, I beseech you look upon us with the favor of a gentleman. We are in a present distress, and utterly unacquainted
in these parts, and therefore forc'd by the calamity of
our misfortune to implore the courtesy, or rather charity,
of those to whom we are strangers.   310

OLIVER.

> Very fine, this!

MERIEL.

> Be, therefore, pleas'd, right noble sir, not only valuing
> us by our outward habits, which cannot but appear
> loathsome or despicable unto you, but as we are forlorn
> Christians, and, in that estimation, be compassionately 315
> moved to cast a handful or two of your silver, or a few of
> your golden pieces unto us, to furnish us with linen, and
> some decent habiliments—

OLIVER.

> They beg as high as the man-beggar I met withal! Sure the
> beggars are all mad today, or bewitched into a language 320
> they understand not. The spirits of some decay'd gentry
> talk in 'em sure.

RACHEL.

> May we expect a gracious answer from you, sir?

MERIEL.

> And that as you can wish our virgin prayers to be propitious
> for you.   325

RACHEL.

> That you never be denied a suit by any mistress.

MERIEL.

> Nay, that the fairest may be ambitious to place their favors
> on you.

RACHEL.

> That your virtue and valor may lead you to the most honor-
> able actions, and that the love of all exquisite ladies may 330
> arm you.

MERIEL.

> And that, when you please to take a wife, may honor,
> beauty, and wealth contend to endow her most with.

RACHEL.

> And that with her you have a long and prosperous
> life.   335

MERIEL.

> A fair and fortunate posterity.

---

323. *gracious*] benevolent.

OLIVER.

This exceeds all that ever I heard, and strikes me into
wonder. Pray, tell me how long have you been beggars,
or how chanc'd you to be so?

RACHEL.

By influence of our stars, sir.   340

MERIEL.

We were born to no better fortune.

OLIVER.

How came you to talk thus, and so much above the beggars'
dialect?

RACHEL.

Our speech came naturally to us, and we ever lov'd to
learn by rote as well as we could.   345

MERIEL.

And to be ambitious above the vulgar, to ask more than
common alms whate'er men please to give us.

OLIVER [aside].

Sure some well disposed gentleman, as myself, got these
wenches. They are too well grown to be mine own, and I
cannot be incestuous with 'em.   350

RACHEL.

Pray, sir, your noble bounty.

OLIVER [aside].

What a tempting lip that little rogue moves there! And
what an enticing eye the t'other. I know not which to
begin with. —What's this, a flea upon thy bosom?

MERIEL.

Is it not a straw-color'd one, sir?   355

OLIVER [aside].

Oh, what a provoking skin is there! That very touch
inflames me.

RACHEL.

Sir, are you mov'd in charity towards us yet?

345. rote] *Brome;* wrote *Q 1–3.*

---

355. *straw-color'd*] i.e., a louse; also signifying "plenty"; the color of
harvested wheat and, therefore, symbolic of "abundance" (so *The Canting
Academy,* edn. 1673, p. 158; and Linthicum, *Costume in the Drama of Shakespeare and his Contemporaries* [1936], p. 45).

OLIVER.

Mov'd? I am mov'd. No flesh and blood more mov'd.

MERIEL.

Then pray, sir, your benevolence.   360

OLIVER [*aside*].

Benevolence? Which shall I be benevolent to, or which
first? I am puzzl'd in the choice. Would some sworn
brother of mine were here to draw a cut with me.

RACHEL.

Sir, noble sir.

OLIVER.

First, let me tell you, damsels, I am bound by a strong 365
vow to kiss all of the woman sex I meet this morning.

MERIEL.

Beggars and all, sir?

OLIVER.

All, all. Let not your coyness cross a gentleman's vow,
I beseech you—   *Kiss.*

RACHEL.

You will tell now.   370

OLIVER.

Tell, quoth-a! I could tell a thousand on those lips—and
as many upon those. —What life-restoring breaths they
have! Milk from the cow steams not so sweetly. I must
lay one of 'em aboard; both if my tackling hold.

RACHEL, MERIEL.

Sir. Sir.   375

OLIVER [*aside*].

But how to bargain, now, will be the doubt. They that beg
so high as by the handfuls, may expect for price above
the rate of good men's wives.

RACHEL.

Now, will you, sir, be pleas'd?

OLIVER.

With all my heart, sweetheart. And I am glad thou knowest 380
my mind. Here is twelvepence apiece for you.

RACHEL, MERIEL.

We thank you, sir.

---

371. *tell a thousand*] i.e., count out in payment.

OLIVER.

That's but in earnest. I'll jest away the rest with ye. Look
here. All this. Come, you know my meaning. Dost thou
look about thee, sweet little one? I like thy care. There's 385
nobody coming. But we'll get behind these bushes. I
know you keep each other's counsels. Must you be drawn
to't? Then I'll pull. Come away—

RACHEL, MERIEL.

Ah, ah—

        Enter Springlove, Vincent, Hilliard.

VINCENT.

Let's beat his brains out.   390

OLIVER.

Come, leave your squealing.

RACHEL.

Oh, you hurt my hand.

HILLIARD.

Or cut the lecher's throat.

SPRINGLOVE.

Would you be hang'd? Stand back. Let me alone.

MERIEL.

You shall not pull us so.   395

SPRINGLOVE.

Oh, do not hurt 'em, master.

OLIVER.

Hurt 'em? I meant 'em but too well. Shall I be so
prevented?

SPRINGLOVE.

They be but young and simple. And if they have offended,
let not your worship's own hands drag 'em to the law, or 400
carry 'em to punishment. Correct 'em not yourself. It is
the beadle's office.

OLIVER.

Do you talk, shake-rag. —Heart, yond's more of 'em. I shall
be beggar-mawl'd if I stay. —Thou say'st right, honest
fellow; there's a tester for thee.   *Exit running.* 405

403. shake-rag] *Q1–2;* shag-rag
Q3.

---

403. *shake-rag*] "Shake" in north country dialect is a disreputable person.
405. *tester*] sixpence.

VINCENT.

He is prevented, and asham'd of his purpose.

SPRINGLOVE.

Nor were we to take notice of his purpose more than to
prevent it.

HILLIARD.

True, politic Springlove. 'Twas better his own fear quit
us of him, than our force. 410

RACHEL.

Look you here, gentlemen, twelvepence apiece.

MERIEL.

Besides fair offers and large promises. What ha' you got
today, gentlemen?

VINCENT.

More than (as we are gentlemen) we would have taken.

HILLIARD.

Yet we put it up in your service. 415

RACHEL, MERIEL.

Ha, ha, ha. Switches and kicks. Ha, ha, ha—

SPRINGLOVE.

Talk not here of your gettings. We must quit this quarter.
The eager gentleman's repulse may arm and return him with
revenge upon us. We must, therefore, leap hedge and ditch
now; through the briers and mires, till we 'scape out of 420
this liberty to our next rendezvous, where we shall meet the
crew, and then, hay toss and laugh all night.

MERIEL.

As we did last night.

RACHEL.

Hold out, Meriel.

MERIEL (*to* Springlove).

Lead on, brave general. 425

VINCENT.

What shall we do? They are in heart still. Shall we go on?

HILLIARD.

There's no flinching back, you see.

SPRINGLOVE.

Besides, if you beg no better than you begin in this lofty
fashion, you cannot 'scape the jail or the whip long.

---

415. *put it up*] endure it, or submit to it.

VINCENT.

To tell you true, 'tis not the least of my purpose to work 430
means for our discovery, to be releas'd out of our trade.

Enter Martin *and* Amie *in poor habits.*

SPRINGLOVE.

Stay, here come more passengers. Single yourselves again,
and fall to your calling discreetly.

HILLIARD.

I'll single no more. If you'll beg in full cry, I am for you.

MERIEL.

Ay, that will be fine; let's charm all together.   435

SPRINGLOVE.

Stay first and list a little.

MARTIN [*to* Amie].

Be of good cheer, sweetheart; we have 'scap'd hitherto, and
I believe that all the search is now retir'd, and we may
safely pass forwards.

AMIE.

I should be safe with thee. But that's a most lying proverb 440
that says, "Where love is, there's no lack." I am faint, and
cannot travel further without meat; and if you lov'd me,
you would get me some.

MARTIN.

We'll venter at the next village to call for some. The
best is, we want no money.   445

AMIE.

We shall be taken then, I fear. I'll rather pine to death.

MARTIN.

Be not so fearful. Who can know us in these clownish
habits?

AMIE.

Our clothes, indeed, are poor enough to beg with. Would
I could beg, so it were of strangers that could not know 450
me, rather than buy of those that would betray us.

MARTIN.

And yonder be some that can teach us.

---

441. *Where . . . lack*] proverbial: In love is no lack (Tilley, L 485).

SPRINGLOVE.

These are the young couple of runaway lovers disguis'd,
that the country is so laid for. Observe and follow now.
—Now the Lord to come with ye, good loving master and   455
mistress; your blessed charity to the poor, lame and
sick, weak and comfortless, that will night and day—

ALL.

Duly and truly pray for you. Duly and truly pray for you.

SPRINGLOVE.

Pray hold your peace, and let me alone. —Good young
master and mistress, a little comfort amongst us all, and   460
to bless you where e'er you go, and—

ALL.

Duly and truly pray for you. Duly and truly—

SPRINGLOVE.

Pray do not use me thus. —Now sweet young master and
mistress, to look upon your poor, that have no relief or
succor, no bread to put in our heads—   465

VINCENT [aside].

Wouldst thou put bread in thy brains?—

All together [*lines* 467–475].

VINCENT.

No lands or livings.

SPRINGLOVE.

No house nor home; nor covering from the cold; no health,
no help but your sweet charity.

MERIEL.

No bands or shirts but lowsie on our backs.   470

HILLIARD.

No smocks or petticoats to hide our scratches.

RACHEL.

No shoes to our legs, or hose to our feet.

VINCENT.

No skin to our flesh, nor flesh to our bones shortly.

HILLIARD [aside].

If we follow the devil that taught us to beg.

467. livings] *Q1–2;* living *Q3.*

---

470. *bands*] wide collars, spreading horizontally from side to side across
the shoulders.

ALL.

Duly and truly pray for you.   475

SPRINGLOVE.

I'll run away from you if you beg a stroke more. —Good
worshipful master and mistress—

MARTIN.

Good friend, forbear. Here is no master or mistress. We
are poor folks. Thou seest no worship upon our backs, I
am sure. And for within, we want as much as you, and 480
would as willingly beg, if we knew how as well.

SPRINGLOVE.

Alack for pity. You may have enough. And what I have
is yours, if you'll accept it. 'Tis wholesome food from a
good gentleman's gate— Alas, good mistress. Much good
do your heart. [*Aside.*]   How savorly she feeds!   485

MARTIN.

What do you mean, to poison yourself?

AMIE.

Do you show love in grudging me?

MARTIN.

Nay, if you think it hurts you not, fall to. I'll not beguile
you. And here, mine host something towards your
reckoning.   490

AMIE.

This beggar is an angel, sure!

SPRINGLOVE.

Nothing by way of bargain, gentle master. 'Tis against
order, and will never thrive. But pray, sir, your reward in
charity.

MARTIN.

Here then, in charity. —This fellow would never make a 495
clerk.

SPRINGLOVE.

What! All this, master?

AMIE.

What is it? Let me see't.

SPRINGLOVE.

'Tis a whole silver threepence, mistress.

492. of bargain] *Q1–2;* of gentle
bargain *Q3.*

AMIE.

For shame, ingrateful miser. Here, friend, a golden crown   500
for thee.

SPRINGLOVE.

Bountiful goodness! Gold? If I thought a dear year were
coming, I would take a farm now.

AMIE.

I have robb'd thy partners of their shares, too. There's a
crown more for them.   505

ALL.

Duly and truly pray for you.

MARTIN [*aside to* Amie].

What have you done? Less would have serv'd. And your
bounty will betray us.

AMIE.

Fie on your wretched policy.

SPRINGLOVE.

No, no, good master. I knew you all this while, and my   510
sweet mistress, too. And now I'll tell you. The search is
every way; the country all laid for you. 'Tis well you
stay'd here. Your habits, were they but a little nearer our
fashion, would secure you with us. But are you married,
master and mistress? Are you joined in matrimony? In   515
heart I know you are. And I will (if it please you) for
your great bounty, bring you to a curate, that lacks no
license, nor has any living to lose, that shall put you together.

MARTIN [*aside*].

Thou art a heavenly beggar!

SPRINGLOVE.

But he is so scrupulous and severely precise, that unless you,   520
mistress, will affirm that you are with child by the gentleman; or that you have, at least, cleft or slept together

506. S.P. ALL] *Brome;* 4. *Q1–3.*

---

500. *golden crown*] five shillings.
    502. *a dear year*] a year when crops are poor and such as do yield bring in
high prices to farmers. See Dekker's *Black Rod* (edn. 1630, sig. B4–B4ᵛ):
"What Covetous Farmer, but is glad of a deere yeare? A dearth of Corne
makes such Cormorants Fat!"; and Robert Greene, *A Quip for an Upstart
Courtier* (ed. Grosart [1881–1886], XI, 285).
    522. *cleft*] past participle of "to cleave" or "to cling to" (*OED*).

(as he calls it), he will not marry you. But if you have
lien together, then 'tis a case of necessity, and he holds
himself bound to do it.   525

MARTIN.

You may say you have.

AMIE.

I would not have it so, nor make that lie against myself
for all the world.

SPRINGLOVE. (*Aside*)

That I like well, and her exceedingly. —I'll do my best
for you, however.   530

MARTIN.

I'll do for thee, that, thou shalt never beg more.

SPRINGLOVE.

That cannot be purchas'd scarce for the price of your
mistress. Will you walk, master? We use no compliments.

AMIE.

By enforc'd matches wards are not set free
So oft, as sold into captivity;   535
Which made me, fearless, fly from one I hate,
Into the hazard of a harder fate.   [*Exeunt.*]

[IV.i]   *Enter* Tallboy, Oliver, *with riding switches.*

TALLBOY.

She's gone. Amie is gone. Ay me, she's gone, and has me
left of joy bereft to make my moan. Oh, me, Amie.

OLIVER.

What the devil ails the fellow, trow? Why! Why, Master
Tallboy, my cousin Tallboy that should'st ha' been, art
not asham'd to cry at this growth? And for a thing that's   5
better lost than found, a wench?

TALLBOY.

Cry! Who cries? Do I cry, or look with a crying counte-
nance? I scorn it, and scorn to think on her but in just
anger.

OLIVER.

So, this is brave now, if 'twould hold.   10

2. my] *Q1–2;* me *Q3.*

TALLBOY.

Nay, it shall hold. And so let her go, for a scurvy what-
d'ee-call't; I know not what bad enough to call her. But
something of mine goes with her, I am sure. She has cost
me in gloves, ribbons, scarfs, rings, and such like things,
more than I am able to speak of at this time. Oh—   15

OLIVER.

Because thou canst not speak for crying. Fie, Master
Tallboy, again?

TALLBOY.

I scorn it again, and any man that says I cry, or will
cry again. And let her go again; and what she has of mine
let her keep, and hang herself, and the rogue that's with   20
her. I have enough, and am heir of a well-known estate,
and that she knows. And, therefore, that she should
slight me, and run away with a wages-fellow, that is but
a petty clerk and a serving-man. There's the vexation of
it. Oh, there's the grief and the vexation of it. Oh—   25

OLIVER.

Now he will cry his eyes out! You, sir. This life have I
had with you all our long journey, which now is at an end
here. This is Master Oldrents' house, where perhaps we
shall find old Hearty, the uncle of that rogue Martin,
that is run away with your sweetheart.   30

TALLBOY.

Ay, 'tis too true, too true, too true. You need not put
me in mind on't. Oh, oh—

OLIVER.

Hold your peace and mind me. Leave your bawling, for fear
I give you correction. This is the house, I say, where it is
most likely we shall hear of your mistress and her com-   35
panion. Make up your face quickly. Here comes one of the
servants, I suppose.

Enter Randall.

Shame not yourself forever, and me for company. Come, be
confident.

25. grief and the] *Q1;* grief and
Q2–3.

TALLBOY.

As confident as yourself or any man. But my poor heart 40
feels what lies here. Here. Ay, here it is. Oh—

OLIVER.

Good morrow, friend. This is Squire Oldrents' house, I
take it.

RANDALL.

Pray, take it not, sir, before it be to be let. It has been
my master's and his ancestors' in that name above these 45
three hundred years, as our house chronicle doth notify,
and not yet to be let. But as a friend, or stranger, in
guestwise, you are welcome to it; as all other gentlemen
are, far and near, to my good master, as you will find anon
when you see him. 50

OLIVER.

Thou speak'st wittily and honestly. But I prithee, good
friend, let our nags be set up; they are tied up at the post.
You belong to the stable, do you not?

RANDALL.

Not so much as the stable belongs to me, sir. I pass through
many offices of the house, sir. I am the running bailie 55
of it.

OLIVER.

We have rid hard, hoping to find the squire at home at this
early time in the morning.

RANDALL.

You are deceiv'd in that, sir. He has been out these four
hours. He is no snail, sir. You do not know him, I perceive, 60
since he has been new molded. But I'll tell you, because
you are gentlemen.

OLIVER.

Our horses, good friend.

RANDALL.

My master is an ancient gentleman, and a great housekeeper; and pray'd for by all the poor in the country. He 65

---

46. *house chronicle*] household book.

55. *running bailie*] i.e., temporary steward or manager of the estate
during absence of Springlove.

60. *no snail*] i.e., no sluggard.

keeps a guest house for all beggars, far and near, costs him
a hundred a year at least, and is as well belov'd among the
rich. But of late, he fell into a great melancholy, upon
what, I know not; for he had then more cause to be merry
than he has now. Take that by the way.   70

OLIVER.

But good friend, our horses.

RANDALL.

For he had two daughters that knew well to order a house
and give entertainment to gentlemen. They were his house-
doves. But now they are flown, and no man knows how,
why, or whither.   75

TALLBOY.

My dove is flown, too. Oh—

RANDALL.

Was she your daughter, sir? She was a young one then, by
the beard you wear.

TALLBOY.

What she was, she was, d'ee see. I scorn to think on her.
But I do. Oh—   80

OLIVER.

Pray hold your peace, or feign some mirth if you can.

TALLBOY (sing).

Let her go, let her go.
I care not if I have her, I have her or no.
Ha, ha, ha. Oh, my heart will break. Oh—

OLIVER.

Pray think of our horses, sir.   85

RANDALL.

This is right my master. When he had his daughters, he
was sad; and now they are gone, he is the merriest man
alive. Up at five o'clock in the morning, and out till
dinner time. Out again at afternoon, and so till supper
time. Skice out this a-way, and skice out that a-way. (He's   90
no snail, I assure you.) And tantivy all the country over,
where hunting, hawking, or any sport is to be made, or

71. friend] *Q2-3;* fiend *Q1.*

---

86. *right*] i.e., just like (Onions).
90. *Skice*] move about quickly.
91. *tantivy*] at full gallop; swiftly.

good fellowship to be had; and so merry upon all occasions,
that you would even bless yourself, if it were possible.

OLIVER.

Our horses, I prithee.   95

RANDALL.

And we, his servants, live as merrily under him, and do all
thrive. I myself was but a silly lad when I came first, a
poor turnspit boy. Gentlemen kept no whirling jacks then,
to cozen poor people of meat. And I have now, without
boast, forty pound in my purse, and am the youngest of half 100
a score in the house, none younger than myself but one; and
he is the steward over all. His name is Master Springlove
(bless him where'er he is). He has a world of means, and
we, the underlings, get well the better by him, besides
the rewards many gentlemen give us that fare well and 105
lodge here sometimes.

OLIVER.

Oh, we shall not forget you, friend, if you remember our
horses before they take harm.

RANDALL.

No hurt, I warrant you; there's a lad walking them.

OLIVER.

Is not your master coming, think you?   110

RANDALL.

He will not be long a-coming. He's no snail, as I told you.

OLIVER.

You told me so, indeed.

RANDALL.

But of all the gentlemen that toss up the ball, yea and
the sack, too, commend me to old Master Hearty, a decay'd
gentleman, lives most upon his own mirth and my master's 115
means, and much good do him with it. He is the finest
companion of all. He does so hold my master up with
stories, and songs, and catches, and t'other cup of sack,
and such tricks and jigs, you would admire. He is with
him now.   120

---

98. *turnspit boy*] boy whose duty it was to turn the spit by the fire.
98. *jacks*] a mechanical device for turning spits.
113. *toss . . . ball*] instigate constant merriment with gay talk, song, and
sack.

OLIVER.

That Hearty is Martin's uncle. I am glad he is here. Bear
up, Tallboy. Now, friend, pray let me ask you a question.
Prithee, stay.

RANDALL.

Nay, marry, I dare not. Your yauds may take cold, and
never be good after it.   *Exit.* 125

OLIVER.

I thought I should never have been rid of him. But no sooner
desir'd to stay, but he is gone. A pretty humor!

                    Enter Randall.

RANDALL.

Gentlemen, my master will be here e'en now, doubt not;
for he is no snail, as I told you.   *Exit.*

OLIVER.

No snail's a great word with him. Prithee, Tallboy, 130
bear up.

                    Enter Usher.

Here comes another gray fellow.

USHER.

Do you stand in the porch, gentlemen? The house is open
to you. Pray enter the hall. I am the usher of it.

OLIVER.

In good time, sir. We shall be bold here, then, to attend 135
your master's coming.

USHER.

And he's upon coming; and when he comes, he comes apace.
He is no snail, I assure you.

OLIVER.

I was told so before, sir. No snail! Sure 'tis the word of
the house, and as ancient as the family.   140

USHER.

This gentleman looks sadly, methinks.

TALLBOY.

Who, I? Not I. Pray pardon my looks for that. But my
heart fells what's what. Ay me—

---

124. *yauds*] mares.
131.1. *Usher*] official household doorkeeper who admits people to the hall
or chamber.

USHER.

Pray walk to the butt'ry, gentlemen. My office leads you
thither.   145

OLIVER.

Thanks, good master usher.

USHER.

I have been usher these twenty years, sir. And have got
well by my place for using strangers respectfully.

OLIVER [aside].

He has given the hint, too.

USHER.

Something has come in by the by, besides standing wages, 150
which is ever duly paid (thank a good master and an honest
steward), Heaven bless 'em. We all thrive under 'em.

Enter Butler *with glasses and a napkin.*

Oh, here comes the butler.

BUTLER.

You are welcome, gentlemen. Please ye draw nearer my
office, and take a morning drink in a cup of sack, if it 155
please you.

OLIVER.

In what please you, sir. We cannot deny the courtesy of
the house in the master's absence.

BUTLER.

He'll come apace when he comes. He's no snail, sir.   *Going.*

OLIVER [aside].

Still 'tis the houseword. And all the servants wear livery- 160
beards.

BUTLER.

Or perhaps you had rather drink white wine and sugar.
Please yourselves, gentlemen; here you may taste all
liquors. No gentleman's house in all this county or the
next so well stor'd (make us thankful for it). And my 165
master, for his hospitality to gentlemen, his charity to the

164. county] *Q1;* Country *Q2-3.*

---

144. *butt'ry*] place for storing liquor; also used for storing provisions.
152.1. *Butler*] servant in charge of the wine cellar who acted as cup
bearer, serving drinks.
160-161. *livery-beards*] beards of the same kind.

poor, and his bounty to his servants, has not his peer in
the kingdom (make us thankful for it). And 'tis as fortunate
a house for servants as ever was built upon fairy-ground.
I, myself, that have serv'd here, man and boy, these 170
four and forty years, have gotten together (besides something, more than I will speak of, distributed among my
poor kin'red) by my wages, my vails at Christmas, and
otherwise, together with my rewards of kind gentlemen that
have found courteous entertainment here—   175

OLIVER [aside].

There he is, too.

BUTLER.

Have, I say, gotten togethĕr (though in a dangerous time I
speak it) a brace of hundred pounds (make me thankful for
it). And for losses, I have had none. I have been butler
these two and thirty years, and never lost the value of a 180
silver spoon, nor ever broke a glass (make me thankful for
it). White wine and sugar, say you, sir?

OLIVER.

Please yourself, sir.

BUTLER.

This gentleman speaks not. Or had you rather take a drink
of brown ale with a toast, or March beer with sugar and 185
nutmeg? Or had you rather drink without sugar?

OLIVER.

Good sir, a cup of your household beer.   *Exit* Butler.
I fear he will draw down to that at last.

Enter Butler *with a silver can of sack.*

BUTLER.

Here, gentlemen, is a cup of my master's small beer, but
it is good old canary, I assure you. And here's to your 190
welcome.

Enter Cook.

COOK.

And welcome the cook says, gentlemen. Brother Butler, lay
a napkin; I'll fetch a cut of the sirloin to strengthen your

---

173. *vails*] a gratuity given to servants, or a tip given by the visitor on his
departure to the servants of the house in which he has been a guest.

patience till my master comes, who will not now be long,
for he's no snail, gentlemen. 195

OLIVER.

I have often heard so. And here's to you, master cook.
—Prithee speak, Master Tallboy, or force one laugh more, if
thou canst.

COOK (*to* Tallboy).

Sir, the cook drinks to you.

TALLBOY.

Ha, ha, ha— 200

OLIVER.

Well said.

TALLBOY.

He is in the same livery-beard, too.

COOK.

But he is the oldest cook, and of the ancientest house,
and the best for housekeeping in this county or the next.
And though the master of it write but squire, I know no 205
lord like him.

Enter Chaplain.

And now he's come. Here comes the word before him.
The parson has ever the best stomach. I'll dish away
presently. *Exit.*

BUTLER.

Is our master come, Sir Domine? 210

CHAPLAIN.

Est ad manum. Non est ille testudo.

OLIVER.

He has the word, too, in Latin. Now bear up, Tallboy.

CHAPLAIN.

Give me a preparative of sack. It is a gentle preparative
before meat. And so a gentle touch of it to you gentlemen.

---

205. *squire*] gentleman next below knight in rank.
210. *Domine*] a clergyman or parson.
211. *Est . . . testudo*] i.e., He is at hand. He is no snail.
213. *preparative of sack*] appetizer; cf. Thomas Heywood's *Philocothonista*
(edn. 1635, sig. G1): "To drinke moderately sharpeneth the appetite,
helpeth digestion, and prepareth the spirits to active mirth and alacritie."
213. *gentle*] excellent.

OLIVER.

It is a gentle offer, sir, and as gently to be taken.   215

Enter Oldrents *and* Hearty.

OLDRENTS.

About with it, my lads. And this is as it should be. —Not
till my turn, sir, I. Though, I confess, I have had but
three morning draughts today.

OLIVER.

Yet it appears you were abroad betimes, sir.

OLDRENTS.

I am no snail, sir.   220

OLIVER.

So your men told us, sir.

OLDRENTS.

But where be my catchers? Come, a round. And so let us
drink.

The catch sung. And they drink about. The singers are all graybeards.

> *A round, a round, a round, boys, a round.*
> *Let mirth fly aloft, and sorrow be drown'd.*   225
> *Old sack, and old songs, and a merry old crew,*
> *Can charm away cares when the ground looks blue.*

OLDRENTS.

Well said, old Hearty. And, gentlemen, welcome.

TALLBOY.

Ah—   *He sighs.*

OLDRENTS.

Oh, mine ears! What was that, a sigh? And in my house? 230
Look, has it not split my walls? If not, make vent for it.
Let it out. I shall be stifled else.   *Exit* Chaplain.

OLIVER.

He hopes your pardon, sir, his cause consider'd.

OLDRENTS.

Cause! Can there be cause for sighing?

---

222. *catchers*] those who sing in a catch.
222. *round*] (1) a quantity of liquor served round a company or drunk off
at one time by each person present; (2) a form of song.
224–227.] music, under the title "A Round" by Mr. William Lawes,
printed in *Catch that Catch Can, or The Musical Companion* (edn. 1667), p. 79.

OLIVER.

He has lost his mistress, sir.   235

OLDRENTS.

Ha, ha, ha. Is that a cause? Do you hear me complain the
loss of my two daughters?

OLIVER.

They are not lost, I hope, sir.

OLDRENTS.

No more can be his mistress. No woman can be lost. They
may be mislaid a little, but found again, I warrant you. 240

TALLBOY.

Ah—   *Sigh.*

OLDRENTS.

'Ods my life! He sighs again, and means to blow me out of
my house. To horse again. Here's no dwelling for me. Or
stay; I'll cure him, if I can. Give him more sack, to drown
his suspirations.   245

While Oldrents *and* Tallboy *drink,* Oliver *takes* Hearty *aside.*

OLIVER.

Sir, I am chiefly to inform you of the disaster.

HEARTY.

May it concern me?

OLIVER.

Your nephew Martin has stol'n my father's ward, that
gentleman's bride that should have been.

HEARTY.

Indeed, sir.   250

OLIVER.

'Tis most true—

He gives Hearty *a letter.*

HEARTY.

Another glass of sack. This gentleman brings good news.

OLIVER.

Sir, if you can prevent his danger—

HEARTY.

Hang all preventions. Let 'em have their destiny.

248. S.P. OLIVER] *Q 2–3;* Old. *Q 1.*

—96—

TALLBOY.

Sir, I should have had her, 'tis true— (*To* Oldrents.) 255
But she is gone, d'e see? And let her go.

OLDRENTS.

Well said. He mends now.

TALLBOY.

I am glad I am rid of her (d'ee see) before I had more to
do with her—

HEARTY.

He mends apace. 260

Hearty *reads the letter.*

TALLBOY.

For should I have married her before she had run away (d'ee
see), and that she had run away (d'ee see) after she had been
married to me (d'ee see), then I had been a married man
without a wife (d'ee see). Where now she being run away
before I am married (d'ee see) I am no more married to her 265
(d'ee see) than she to me (d'ee see). And so long as I am
none of hers (d'ee see) nor she none of mine (d'ee see), I
ought to care as little for her, now she is run away (d'ee
see), as if she had stay'd with me, d'ee see.

OLDRENTS.

Why this is excellent! Come hither, Hearty. 270

TALLBOY.

I perceive it now, and the reason of it; and how, by con-
sequence (d'ee see) I ought not to look any further after
her. (*Cries.*) But that she should respect a poor base
fellow, a clerk at the most and a serving-man at best, before
me, that am a rich man at the worst and a gentleman at 275
least, makes me—I know not what to say—

OLDRENTS.

Worse than ever 'twas! Now he cries outright.

TALLBOY.

I know not what to say—what to say—oh—

HEARTY.

Then I do, sir. The poor base fellow that you speak of is
my nephew, as good a gentleman as yourself. I understand 280
the business by your friend here.

273. her] *Q1; not in Q2–3.*

TALLBOY.

I cry you mercy, sir.

OLDRENTS.

You shall cry no mercy, nor anything else here, sir; nor
for anything here, sir. This is no place to cry in. Nor
for any business. —(*To* Oliver.) You, sir, that come on 285
business—

OLIVER.

It shall be none, sir.

OLDRENTS.

My house is for no business but the belly-business. You
find not me so uncivil, sir, as to ask you from whence you
came, who you are, or what's your business. I ask you no 290
question. And can you be so discourteous as to tell me or
my friend anything like business. If you come to be merry
with me, you are welcome. If you have any business,
forget it; you forget where you are else. And so to dinner.

HEARTY.

Sir, I pray let me only prevail with you but to read this. 295

OLDRENTS.

Spoil my stomach now, and I'll not eat this fortnight.

He reads aside.

HEARTY [*to* Oliver].

While he reads, let me tell you, sir. That my nephew Martin
has stol'n that gentleman's mistress, it seems, is true.
But I protest, as I am a gentleman, I know nothing of the
matter, nor where he or she is. But as I am the foresaid 300
gentleman, I am glad on't with all my heart. Ha! my boy
Mat. Thou shalt restore our house.

OLIVER.

Let him not hear, to grieve him, sir.

HEARTY.

Grieve him? What should he do with her; teach their
children to cry? 305

TALLBOY.

But I do hear you though; and I scorn to cry, as much as
you (d'ee see), or your nephew either (d'ee see).

HEARTY.

Now thou art a brave fellow. So, so, hold up thy head, and
thou shalt have a wife, and a fine thing.

TALLBOY.

Hang a wife, and pax o' your fine thing (d'ee see); I scorn 310
your fopperies, d'ee see.

OLDRENTS.

And I do hear thee, my boy; and rejoice in thy conversion.
If thou canst but hold now.

TALLBOY.

Yes, I can hold, sir. And I hold well with your sack. I
could live and die with it, as I am true Tallboy.   315

OLDRENTS.

Now thou art a tall fellow, and shalt want no sack.

TALLBOY.

And, sir, I do honor you (d'ee see) and should wish myself
one of your household servants (d'ee see) if I had but a
gray beard; d'ee see? "Hey," as old Master Clack says.

OLDRENTS.

Well, I have read the business here.   320

OLIVER.

Call it not business, I beseech you, sir. We defy all business.

TALLBOY.

Ay, marry do we, sir. D'ee see, sir? "And a hey," as old
Master Clack says.

OLDRENTS.

Grammercy sack. Well, I have read the matter here written
by Master Clack. And do but bear up in thy humor, I will 325
wait upon thee home.

Knock within.

Hark! They knock to the dresser. I have heard much of
this old odd-ceited Justice Clack; and now I long to see
him. 'Tis but crossing the country two days and a night's
journey. We'll but dine and away presently. Bear up, I 330
say, Master Tallboy.

---

316. *tall*] stout, brave.

327. *knock . . . dresser*] The dresser was a table in the dining hall from
which dishes were served; hence a form of warning that dinner is to be
served. Cf. Brome's *Northern Lass*, V.ix: "All the unquietnesse will be in the
Kitchin presently. If your meat stay for you, Gallants. *Knock within.* Twas
time to speak. They knock at Dresser already. Will yee in?"

328. *odd-ceited*] i.e., odd-conceited or whimsical.

TALLBOY.

I will bear up, I warrant you, d'ee see, sir. But here's a
grudging still—   *Exeunt.*

[IV.ii]

A great noise within of rude music, laughing, singing, &c. Enter Amie,
Rachel, Meriel.

AMIE.

Here's a wedding with a witness, and a holiday with a
hoigh. Let us out of the noise, as we love our ears.

RACHEL.

Yes, and here we may pursue our own discourse, and hear
one another.

MERIEL.

Concerning Springlove and yourself, Mistress Amie.   5

AMIE.

Well, ladies, my confidence in you, that you are the same
that you have protested yourselves to be, hath so far won
upon me that I confess myself well affected both to the
mind and person of that Springlove. And if he be (as
fairly you pretend) a gentleman, I shall easily dispense   10
with fortune.

RACHEL, MERIEL.

He is, upon our honors.

AMIE.

How well that high engagement suits your habits.

RACHEL.

Our minds and blood are still the same.

AMIE.

I have pass'd no affiance to the other   15
That stole me from my guardian and the match
He would have forc'd me to, from which I would
Have fled with any, or without a guide.
Besides, his mind, more clownish than his habit,
Deprav'd by covetousness and cowardice,   20
Forc'd me into a way of misery
To take relief from beggars.

MERIEL.   From poor us.

---

2. *hoigh*] excitement.

AMIE.

And then, to offer to marry me under a hedge as the old
couple were today, without book or ring, by the chaplain of
the beggars' regiment, your patrico, only to save charges.   25

RACHEL.

I have not seen the wretch these three hours. Whither is
he gone?

AMIE.

He told me to fetch horse and fit raiment for us, and
so to post me hence. But I think it was to leave me on
your hands.   30

MERIEL.

He has taken some great distaste sure, for he is damnable
jealous.

RACHEL.

Ay, didst thou mark what a wild look he cast when Springlove tumbled her and kiss'd her on the straw this morning,
while the music play'd to the old wedding-folks?   35

MERIEL.

Yes, and then Springlove, to make him madder, told him
that he would be his proxy and marry her for him, and lie
with her the first night with a naked cudgel betwixt 'em, and
make him a king of beggars.

AMIE.

I saw how it anger'd him. And I imagin'd then and before   40
that there was more in Springlove than downright beggar.
But though he be never so good a gentleman, he shall
observe fit time and distance till we are married.

RACHEL.

Matrimony forbid else. —(She's taken.)— But while we
talk of a match towards, we are miss'd within in the bride-   45
barn among the revel-rout.

AMIE.

We have had all the sport they could make us in the past
passages.

MERIEL.

How cautious the old contracted couple were for portion
and jointure!   50

---

23. *under a hedge*] See "The Persons of the Play," l. 21, note.

RACHEL.

What feoffees, she being an heir of fourscore (and seven
years stone-blind) had, in trust for her estate.

AMIE.

And how carefully he secur'd all to himself, in case he
outliv'd her, being but seven years older than she. And
what pains the lawyer of the rout here took about it.   55

RACHEL.

And then, how solemnly they were join'd, and admonish'd
by our Parson Under-hedge to live together in the fear of
the lash, and give good example to the younger reprobates,
to beg within compass, to escape the jaws of the justice,
the clutch of the constable, the hooks of the headborough,   60
and the biting blows of the beadle. And, in so doing,
they should defy the devil and all his works, and after their
painful pilgrimage in this life, they should die in the
ditch of delight.

MERIEL.

Oh, but poet Scribble's Epithalamium.   65

> *To the blind virgin of fourscore,*
>   *And the lame bachelor of more,*
> *How Cupid gave her eyes to see,*
>   *And Vulcan lent him legs;*
> *How Venus caus'd their sport to be*   70
>   *Prepar'd with butter'd eggs.*
> *Yet when she shall be seven years wed,*
>   *She shall be bold to say,*
> *She has as much her maidenhead,*
>   *As on her wedding day.*   75

RACHEL.

So may some wives that were married at sixteen, to lads
of one and twenty.

---

60. *hooks*] pitchfork-like instruments with barbed springs at side used in
making arrests.

60. *headborough*] a parish officer with duties identical to those of the
petty constable.

71. *butter'd eggs*] regarded as an aphrodisiac.

AMIE.

But at the wedding feast, when the bride bridled it and
her groom saddled it! There was the sport, in her mumping
and his champing, the crew scrambling, ourselves trembling;   80
then the confusion of noises in talking, laughing, scolding,
singing, howling; with their actions of snatching, scratching,
tousing and lousing themselves, and one another—

Enter Springlove, Vincent, *and* Hilliard.

But who comes here?

SPRINGLOVE.

Oh, ladies, you have lost as much mirth as would have fill'd   85
up a week of holidays.

Springlove *takes* Amie *aside and courts her in a gentle way.*

VINCENT.

I am come about again for the beggar's life now.

RACHEL.

You are. I am glad on't.

HILLIARD.

There is no life but it.

VINCENT.

With them there is no grievance or perplexity;   90
No fear of war, or state disturbances.
No alteration in a commonwealth,
Or innovation, shakes a thought of theirs.

MERIEL.

Of ours, you should say.

HILLIARD.   Of ours, he means.

We have no fear of lessening our estates;   95

---

78. *bridled*] pun: (1) gesture "To throw up the head and draw in the
chin expressing pride, vanity" (*OED*); (2) play on "bride," meaning to
play the bride (Onions).

79. *saddled*] "to bestride" (*OED*), i.e., brought under control.

79. *mumping*] north country dialect for chewing, gnawing greedily
(Wright).

80. *champing*] noisily munching the food.

83. *tousing*] "To pull (a woman) about rudely, indelicately, or in horse-
play; to tousle" (*OED*).

93. *innovation*] "revolution" (*OED*); here with the suggestion of the
pending civil war between parliament and king.

Nor any grudge with us (without taxation)
To lend or give, upon command, the whole
Strength of our wealth for public benefit;
While some, that are held rich in their abundance,
(Which is their misery, indeed) will see 100
Rather a general ruin upon all,
Than give a scruple to prevent the fall.

VINCENT.

'Tis only we that live.

RACHEL.

I'm glad you are so taken with your calling.

MERIEL.

We are no less, I assure you. We find the sweetness of 105
it now.

RACHEL.

The mirth, the pleasure, the delights. No ladies live
such lives.

MERIEL.

Some few, upon necessity, perhaps. But that's not worth
gramercy. 110

VINCENT [aside].

They will never be weary.

HILLIARD [aside].

Whether we seem to like or dislike, all's one to them.

VINCENT [aside].

We must do something to be taken by and discovered; we
shall never be ourselves and get home again else.

Springlove *and* Amie *come to the rest.*

SPRINGLOVE.

I am yours forever. [*To the others.*] —Well, ladies, you 115
have miss'd rare sport; but now the bride has miss'd you
with her half-half eye, and the bridegroom, with the help
of his crutches, is drawing her forth for a dance here in
the opener air. The house is now too hot for 'em.

[*Enter* Bride, Groom, Soldier, Courtier, Lawyer, Poet.]

Oh, here come the chief revelers, the soldier, the courtier, 120
the lawyer, and the poet, who is master of their revels,
before the old couple in state. Attend and hear him
speak as their inductor.

POET.

Here, on this green, like king and queen,
    (For a short truce) we do produce   125
Our old new-married pair.
Of dish and wallet, and of straw pallet,
    With rags to show from top to toe,
She is the ancient heir.

He is the lord of bottle-gourd   130
Of satchel great for bread and meat,
    And for small pence, a purse.
To all that give, "Long may you live,"
    He loudly cries; but who denies
Is sure to have his curse.   135

VINCENT.

Well said, field-poet. Phoebus, we see, inspires
As well the beggar as the poet laureate.

SPRINGLOVE.

And shines as warm under a hedge-bottom as on the tops
of palaces.

POET.

I have not done yet. Now this is to incite you to dance.   140

Prepare yourselves, like fairy elves,
    Now in a dance to show
That you approve the god of love
    Has many shafts to's bow;

With golden head, and some of lead,   145
    But that which made these feel,
By subtle craft, was sure a shaft
    That headed was with steel.

For they were old, no earth more cold;
    Their hearts were flints entire;   150
Whence the steel's stroke did sparks provoke,
    That set their bloods on fire.

Now strike up piper; and each lover here
Be blithe, and take his mistress by the goll.

---

127. *dish and wallet*] a wooden receptacle for alms and beggar's bag.
130. *bottle-gourd*] a flask-like gourd.
143. *approve*] acknowledge.   154. *goll*] hand.

HILLIARD.

    That's no rhyme, poet.   155

POET.

    There's as good poetry in blank verse, as meter.   *Music.*

SPRINGLOVE.

    Come, hey! the dance, the dance. Nay, we'll ha' the old
couple in, as blind and lame as they are.

BRIDE.

    What will you so?   *Dance.*

SPRINGLOVE.

    Well hobbled, bridegroom!   160

VINCENT.

    Well grop'd, bride!

HILLIARD.

    Hey, lusty. Hey-holiday.

SPRINGLOVE.

    Set 'em down; set 'em down. They ha' done well.

GROOM.

    Aha! I am lustier than I was thirty years ago.

BRIDE.

    And I, than I was threescore past. Ahem, ahem.   165

VINCENT.

    What a night here's towards!

HILLIARD.

    Sure they will kill one another.

POET.

    Each with a fear the t'other will live longest.

SPRINGLOVE.

    Poet, thou hast spoken learnedly and acted bravely.
Thou are both poet and actor.   170

POET.

    So has been many famous men. And if here were no worse,
we might have a masque or a comedy presented tonight, in
honor of the old couple.

VINCENT.

    Let us each man try his ability upon some subject now
extempore.   175

SPRINGLOVE.

    Agreed. Give us a theme, and try our action.

POET.

I have already thought upon't. I want but actors.

HILLIARD.

What persons want you? What would you present?

POET.

I would present a commonwealth: Utopia,
With all her branches and consistencies.   180

RACHEL.

I'll be Utopia; who must be my branches?

POET.

The country, the city, the court, and the camp, epitomiz'd
and personated by a gentleman, a merchant, a courtier, and
a soldier.

SOLDIER.

I'll be your soldier. Am not I one? Ha!   185

COURTIER.

And am not I a fashionable courtier?

POET.

But who the citizen or merchant?

SPRINGLOVE.

I.

VINCENT.

And I your country gentleman.

HILLIARD.

Or I.   190

POET.

Yet to our moral I must add two persons, Divinity and Law.

LAWYER.

Why la you now, and am not I a lawyer?

POET.

But where's Divinity?

VINCENT.

Marry, that I know not. One of us might do that, if either
knew how to handle it.   195

SPRINGLOVE.

Where's the old patrico, our priest, my ghostly father?
He'll do it rarely.

1 BEGGAR.

He was telling fortunes e'en now to country wenches. I'll
fetch him.   *Exit.*

SPRINGLOVE [to Amie].

That Patrico I wonder at; he has told me strange things 200
in clouds.

AMIE.

And me somewhat that I may tell you hereafter.

SPRINGLOVE.

That you shall be my bride?

AMIE.

I will not tell you now.

VINCENT.

Well; but what must our speeches tend to? What must we 205
do one with another?

POET.

I would have the country, the city, and the court, be at
great variance for superiority. Then would I have
Divinity and Law stretch their wide throats to appease
and reconcile them; then would I have the soldier cudgel 210
them all together and overtop them all. Stay, yet I want
another person.

HILLIARD.

What must he be?

POET.

A beggar.

VINCENT.

Here's enough of us, I think. What must the beggar do?   215

POET.

He must at last overcome the soldier, and bring them all
to Beggars' Hall. And this, well acted, will be for the
honor of our calling.

ALL.

A Scribble! A Scribble!

HILLIARD.

Come, where's this patrico, that we may begin?   220

Enter Patrico.

PATRICO.

Alack and welladay,
This is no time to play.

221–222.] *one line in Q 1.*

---

219. *A Scribble*] i.e., a hasty contriver of masques; see II.i.272, note.

Our quarter is beset.
We are all in the net.
Leave off your merry glee.   225

VINCENT.

You begin scurvily.

SPRINGLOVE.

Why, what's the matter?

WITHIN.

Bing awast, bing awast. The queer cove and the harman-
beck.

Some Beggars *run over the stage.*

SPRINGLOVE.

We are beset indeed. What shall we do?   230

VINCENT.

I hope we shall be taken.

HILLIARD.

If the good hour be come, welcome by the grace of good
fortune.

Enter Sentwell, Constable, *Watch. The crew slip away.*

SENTWELL.

Beset the quarter round. Be sure that none escape.

SPRINGLOVE.

Lord to come with you, blessed master, to a many distressed— 235

VINCENT, HILLIARD.

Duly and truly pray for you.

RACHEL, MERIEL.

Good your good worship, duly and truly, &c.

SENTWELL.

A many counterfeit rogues! So frolic and so lamentable
all in a breath? You were acting a play but now. We'll
act with you. Incorrigible vagabonds.   240

223–224.] *one line in Q1.*

---

228. *Bing awast*] i.e., Hie you hence (*Eng. Vil.*, sig. O2^v).
228. *queer cove*] Justice of Peace (*Eng. Vil.*, sig. N2^v).
228–229. *harman-beck*] constable (*Eng. Vil.*, sig. N4).

SPRINGLOVE.

Good master, 'tis a holiday with us. An heir was married
here today.

SENTWELL.

Married! Not so, I hope. Where is she? 'Tis for an heir
we seek.

SPRINGLOVE.

Here she is, master. —Hide yourselves in the straw—the 245
straw. Quickly into the straw—

SENTWELL.

What tell'st thou me of this? An old blind beggar-woman.
We must find a young gentlewoman-heir among you.
Where's all the rest of the crew?

CONSTABLE.

Slipp'd into the barn and the bushes by, but none can 'scape. 250

SENTWELL.

Look you to that, and to these here.   *Exit with Watch.*

SPRINGLOVE.

Into the straw, I say.

VINCENT.

No, good Springlove. The ladies and we are agreed now
to draw stakes, and play this lousy game no further.

HILLIARD.

We will be taken, and disclose ourselves. You see we shall be 255
forc'd to it else. The cowardly clerk has done't to save
himself.

SPRINGLOVE.

Do you fear no shame, ladies?

RACHEL.

Dost think it a shame to leave begging?

MERIEL.

Or that our father will turn us out to it again?   260

SPRINGLOVE.

Nay, since you are so resolute, know that I, myself, begin
to find this is no course for gentlemen. This lady shall
take me off it.

AMIE.

Make but your protestations good, and take me yours. And
for the gentleman that surprises us, though he has all my 265
uncle's trust, he shall do anything for me to our advantage.

VINCENT.

> If, Springlove, thou could'st post now to thy tiring-house
> and fetch all our clothes, we might get off most neatly.

SPRINGLOVE.

> A horse and six hours' travel would do that.

AMIE.

> You shall be furnish'd, doubt not.   270

> *Enter* Sentwell, *Watch.*

SENTWELL.

> She's scap'd or is invisible. You, sir, I take to be the
> chief rogue of this regiment. Let him be whipp'd till he
> brings forth the heir.

CONSTABLE.

> That is but till he stinks, sir. Come, sir, strip, strip.

AMIE.

> Unhand him, sir. What heir do you seek, Master Sentwell? 275

SENTWELL.

> Precious, how did my haste oversee her? Oh, Mistress Amie!
> Could I or your uncle, Justice Clack, a wiser man than I,
> ever ha' thought to have found you in such company?

AMIE.

> Of me, sir, and my company, I have a story to delight you,
> which on our march towards your house, I will relate to you. 280

SENTWELL.

> And thither will I lead you as my guest.
> But to the law surrender all the rest.
> I'll make your peace.

AMIE.   We must fare all alike.   *Exeunt.*

[V.i]   [*Enter*] Clack, Martin.

CLACK.

> I have forgiven you. Provided that my niece be safely
> taken, and so to be brought home. Safely, I say; that
> is to say, unstain'd, unblemish'd, undishonor'd; that is to

---

267. *tiring-house*] dressing room.
276. *Precious*] an expletive for God's "precious blood" or "precious
body" (*OED*).

-111-

say, with no more faults, criminal or accusative, than
those she carried with her.   5

MARTIN.

Sir, I believe—

CLACK.

Nay, if we both speak together, how shall we hear one
another? You believe her virtue is armor of proof without
your counsel or your guard, and therefore you left her
in the hands of rogues and vagabonds to make your own   10
peace with me. You have it. Provided, I say (as I said
before) that she be safe; that is to say, uncorrupted,
undefiled; that is to say—as I said before—

MARTIN.

Mine intent, sir, and my only way—

CLACK.

Nay, if we both speak together, how shall we hear one   15
another, as I said before? Your intent, and your only way,
you would ha' said, was to run away with her; and that by
her only instigation to avoid the tie of marriage with
Master Tallboy; that is to say, to shun the match that I had
made for her; that is to say, rather to disobey me than to   20
displease herself. Wherein (although she did not altogether
transgress the law) she did both offend and prejudice me,
an instrument, nay, I may say, a pillar thereof. And you,
in assisting her, furthering, and conveying her away, did
not only infringe the law in an unlawful departure from   25
your master, but in a higher point; that is to say, top
and top-gallows high. I would ha' found a jury should ha'
found it so.

MARTIN.

But, sir, an't please you.

CLACK.

Must we then both speak together? Have I not borne with   30
thee, to speak all thou pleasest in thy defense? Have I
not broke mine own rule, which is to punish before I
examine, and so to have the law the surer o' my side? And

19–20. had made for] *Q1;* hade for
Q2; had for *Q3.*

4. *accusative*] i.e., accusatory.

dost thou still persist? Hold your own peace; or, as I am
a justice of the king's, I will unsay what I said before   35
and set a *Currat Lex* at you, sirrah, that shall course you
up the heavy hill. Oh, is your tongue fallen into your leg
now? Do not you know I have acquitted you? Provided—
as I said before. Go your way in, and see that the gentlemen,
who, I think, were got in sack, christen'd in sack, nursed   40
with sack, and fed up to gray hairs with only sack; see, I
say, that they want no sack. My son Oliver (I thank him)
has brought me a pair of such guests.

Enter Sentwell.

Oh, Master Sentwell! Good news?

SENTWELL.

Of beggarly news, the best you have heard.   45

CLACK.

That is to say, you have found my niece among the beggars.
That is to say—

SENTWELL.

True, Sir Oliver, I found her—

CLACK.

Now if we both speak together, who shall hear one another?

SENTWELL.

I thought your desire was to be inform'd.   50

CLACK.

I can inform myself, sir, by your looks. I have taken a
hundred examinations i' my days of felons, and other
offenders, out of their very countenances; and wrote 'em
down verbatim to what they would have said. I am sure it
has serv'd to hang some of 'em, and whip the rest.   55

SENTWELL.

Justice Clack still! He must talk all. His clack must only
go.

CLACK.

But to the point. You have found my niece. You have left
her at your own house; not only to shift her out of her

53. wrote] *Q1–2;* wrought *Q3.*

---

36. *Currat Lex*] legal term for maximum penalty.
57. *go*] i.e., go on or be allowed to go on.

disguise, but out of her shame, to come nearer me, until I   60
send her pardon.

SENTWELL.

Most true, sir. But the company she was in—

CLACK.

Again! Do not I know the company? Beggars, rogues,
vagabonds, and hedge-birds.

SENTWELL.

But do you know whom, or how many we have taken? And   65
how the rest escap'd?

CLACK.

A needless knowledge. Why should we take more than
herself? Or how could you take those that could escape?

Enter Martin.

MARTIN.

Sir, the old gentlemen within sent me to wait upon you.
Without you (they say) they need not my service.   70

CLACK.

Tell 'em then I'll wait on 'em presently.   *Exit* Martin.

SENTWELL.

But sir, we have taken with her such beggars, such rogues,
such vagabonds, and such hedge-birds (since you call 'em
so) as you never knew, or heard of, though now the countries
swarm with 'em under every hedge, as if an innumerable   75
army of 'em were lately disbanded without pay. Hedge-birds,
said you? Hedge-ladybirds, hedge-cavaliers, hedge-soldier,
hedge-lawyer, hedge-fiddlers, hedge-poet, hedge-players,
and a hedge-priest among 'em. Such we have taken for the
principals. But to see how the multitude 'scap'd us was   80
more sport than pity. How, upon a watchword given,
they in the instant vanish'd by more several ways than there
were legs among 'em; how the cripples leap'd over pales
and hedges; how the blind found their way through lakes and
ditches; how a doxy flew with two children at her back,   85
and two more, perhaps, in her belly—

CLACK.

A hedge-priest have you taken, say you?

---

83. *pales*] fence or enclosing barriers.

SENTWELL.

    Yes, sir, an old patrico, an ancient prophet, to tell
fortunes and cozen our poor country people of their single
money.   90

Enter Oliver.

OLIVER.

    Sir, Master Oldrents, in that he enjoys not your company
begins to doubt of his welcome.

CLACK.

    Who led him into that doubt? I, or you that brought him
hither?

OLIVER.

    Sir, his own desire and love to you brought him hither. I   95
but show'd him the way.

CLACK.

    You reason fairly. Tell him I come.

OLIVER.

    Pray, sir, be pleas'd to do so, for he says—

CLACK.

    Nay, if we both talk together—

OLIVER.

    Who shall hear one another.   *Exit* Oliver.   100

CLACK.

    But are there players among the apprehended?

SENTWELL.

    Yes, sir. And they were contriving to act a play among
themselves, just as we surpris'd 'em and spoil'd their sport.

CLACK.

    Players! I'll pay them above all the rest.

SENTWELL.

    You shall do well in that, to put 'em in stock to set up   105
again.

CLACK.

    Yes, I'll put 'em in stocks, and set 'em up to the whipping-
post. They can act justices, can they? I'll act a justice

   89–90. *single money*] single coins (J. O. Halliwell, *Dictionary of Archaic
and Provincial Words*, London, 1924).

   105. *put . . . stock*] pun: (1) provide with a stock of merchandise and set
up in business, (2) confinement in stocks as a punishment.

among 'em; that is to say, I will do justice upon them; that is to say— 110

SENTWELL.

Pray sir, be not severe; they act kings and emperors, as well as justices. And justice is blind they say: you may therefore be pleas'd to wink a little. I find that you have merry old gentlemen in your house that are come far to visit you. I'll undertake that these players, with the help 115 of their poet, in a device which they have already studied, and a pack of clothes which I shall supply 'em with, shall give your guests much content, and move compassion in you towards the poor strolls.

function of players [margin note]

CLACK.

But you know my way of justice (and that's a sure way) is 120 to punish 'em first, and be compassionate afterwards, as I find 'em upon their examination.

SENTWELL.

But for your guests' sakes, who (I know) do favor and affect the quality of actors very much, permit 'em, sir. It will enlarge your entertainment exceedingly. 125

CLACK.

And perhaps save me the expense of a runlet of sack the while. Well, sir, for that respect, and upon your undertaking that they shall please, I will prorogue my justice on the rogues. And so to my merry gentlemen, whom I will prepare to see their interlude against after supper. But pray, 130 Master Sentwell, as you have found my niece, look to her and see her decently brought home.

SENTWELL.

In her own best apparel. But you must prorogue your displeasure to her, too.

CLACK.

I will do so, until my scarce welcome guests be gone. 135

---

116. *device*] a masque or dramatic presentation.
119. *strolls*] i.e., strollers, those who roam from place to place with no settled habitation.
124. *quality*] profession.
126. *runlet*] a cask of liquor. "Large runlets appear usually to have varied between 12 and 18½ gallons, small ones between a pint or quart and three or four gallons" (*OED*).
128. *prorogue*] defer, postpone.
130. *against*] in anticipation of.

Enter Randall.

RANDALL.

Sir, my master sends you word, and plainly, that without
your company, your entertainment stinks. He has commanded me saddle his nags and away tonight. If you come
not at once, twice, thrice, he's gone presently, before supper.
He'll find an host at an inn worth a hundred o' you.   140

CLACK.

Good friend, I will now satisfy your master, without telling
him he has a saucy knave to his man.   *Exit* Clack.

RANDALL.

Thank your worship.

SENTWELL.

Do you hear, friend, you serve Master Oldrents.

RANDALL.

I could ha' told you that. And the best housekeeper my 145
master is of any gentleman in the county he dwells in; and
the best master to a man, as I, the worst of twenty, can
say for him, and would be asham'd to say less.

SENTWELL.

Your name is Randall.

RANDALL.

Forgi' me! Are you so wise? You are too young to be my 150
godsire. And I hope not old enough to be a witch. How
know you that I am Randall? Were you ever at my master's
house i' Nottinghamshire, or at Dunghillford, where I was
born?

SENTWELL.

No. But I have notes to know you by.   155

RANDALL.

I was never twelve mile from thence i' my life before this
journey. God send me within ken of our own kitchen smoke
again.

SENTWELL.

Your master's steward's name is Springlove.

RANDALL.

Master Springlove, an't please you. There is not an honester 160
gentleman between this and the head of him. And my
heart's with him, where'er he is. Know you him, too?

---

155. *notes*] "knowledge, information" (*OED*).

SENTWELL.

Yes, and your master's daughters, too.

RANDALL.

Whaw.

SENTWELL.

And that they are all from home, your master knows not 165
where.

RANDALL.

Whaw, whaw. Know you that, too?

SENTWELL.

Yes, and the two young gentlemen that are with 'em, Master
Vincent and Master Hilliard.

RANDALL.

Whaw, whaw again. You know 'em all, I think. But know 170
you where they all are?

SENTWELL.

Even here by, at my own house.

RANDALL.

Whaw—

SENTWELL.

And they knowing that your master is here, and Master
Hearty, too—   175

RANDALL.

Whaw, whaw.

SENTWELL.

And yourself, too. They directed me to find you, Randall,
and bring you to 'em.

RANDALL.

Whaw, whaw, whaw, whaw—why do we not go then?

SENTWELL.

But secretly. Not a word to anybody.   180

RANDALL.

Mum. Will you go then?

Enter Martin.

MARTIN.

Oh, Master Oldrents' man. Pray let me entreat you into
the buttery.

RANDALL [*ignoring* Martin].

Will you go, Master Gentleman?

MARTIN.

Indeed it is my master's desire, and he commanded me.   185

RANDALL.

Now, when it's supper-time, did he? To fill my belly with
thin drink to save his meat? It's the manner in churls'
houses. —Will you go, Master Gentleman?

MARTIN.

In troth, my master is so merry with yours within—

RANDALL.

Shit o' your master. My master's steward's a better man.   190
I'll to him at this gentleman's house and all the rest.
Whaw, whaw—

SENTWELL.

Randall, you forget.

RANDALL.

Mum again then. Why would you not go then?

Exeunt Sentwell *and* Randall.

MARTIN.

The man's as mad as his master. The strangest strangers 195
that ever came to our house.

Enter Tallboy.

TALLBOY.

Well, Martin, for confessing thy fault, and the means thou
mad'st whereby she is taken, I am friends with thee. But
I shall never look upon her, or thee, but with grief of mind,
however I bear it outwardly. Oh—   200

MARTIN.

You bear it very manfully, methinks.

TALLBOY.

Ay, you think so, and I know so— But what I feel, I feel.
Would one of us two had never both seen one another. Oh—

MARTIN.

You speak very good sense, sir. But does my master continue
his merry humor with the old gentlemen within?   205

194.1. *Exeunt*] *this   edition;   Exit*   203. both] *Q 1; not in Q 2–3.*
Q 1–3.

---

187. *churls*] misers'.

TALLBOY.

Yes, Justice Clack's clack goes as merrily as any.

MARTIN.

Well said, sir. Now you speak merrily, too. But I could say
somewhat that would still him. And for your comfort, I'll tell
you. Mistress Amie is fallen in love with one of the beggars.

TALLBOY.

Then have I nothing else to do, but to laugh at thee as 210
long as I live. Ha, ha, ha— To let a beggar cozen thee
of her. Ha, ha, ha. A beggar! I shall die merrily yet.
Ha, ha, ha.

Enter Clack, Oldrents, Hearty, Oliver.

CLACK.

A-hey, boys, a-hey. This is right; that is to say, as I would
have it; that is to say— 215

TALLBOY.

A beggar. Ha, ha, ha—

MARTIN.

Ha, ha, ha—

CLACK.

A-hey, boys, a-hey. They are as merry without, as we were
within. A-hey, Master Oldrents and Master Hearty! The
virtue of your company turns all to mirth and melody, with 220
a-hey trololly lolly lolly. Is't not so, Master Hearty?

OLDRENTS.

Why thus it should be. How was I deceiv'd! Now I see you
are a good fellow.

OLIVER.

He was never so before. If it be a lightning before death,
the best is, I am his heir. 225

TALLBOY, MARTIN.

Ha, ha, ha—

CLACK.

Again, boys, again; that is to say, a-hey, boys, a-hey—

HEARTY.

What is the motive of your mirth, Nephew Martin? Let us
laugh with you.

OLDRENTS.

Was that spoke like my friend, Hearty? Lack we motives to 230
laugh? Are not all things, anything, everything to be

laugh'd at? And if nothing were to be seen, felt, heard,
or understood, we would laugh at it, too.

CLACK.

You take the loss of your mistress merrily, Master
Tallboy.   235

TALLBOY.

More merrily than you will take the finding of her. Ha, ha,
ha. A beggar! Ha, ha, ha—

CLACK.

Can I be sad to find her, think you?

MARTIN.

He thinks you will be displeas'd with her and chide her.

CLACK.

You are deceiv'd, Master Tallboy; you are wide, Master 240
Tallboy, above half your length, Master Tallboy. Law and
justice shall sleep, and mirth and good fellowship ride a
circuit here tonight. A-hey, Master Oldrents; a-hey, Master
Hearty; and a-hey, Son Oliver; and a-hey, Nephew Tallboy
that should ha' been, and a-hey, my Clerk Martin; and a- 245
hey for the players. When come they? Son Oliver, see for
Master Sentwell, that is no readier with his new company.

TALLBOY.

Players! Let us go see, too. I never saw any players.

                                    Exeunt Tallboy, Martin.

OLIVER.

This is the first fit that ever he had of this disease. And
if it be his last, I say, as I said before, I am his heir. *Exit.* 250

OLDRENTS.

But is there a play to be expected, and acted by beggars?

CLACK.

That is to say, by vagabonds; that is to say, by strolling
players. They are upon their purgation. If they can present
anything to please you, they may escape the law; that
is (a-hey). If not, tomorrow, gentlemen, shall be acted 255

---

241. above . . . Tallboy] *Q1; not in*
Q2–3.
247. Sentwell, that] *Q1;* Sentwell,
that Sentwell, that *Q2–3.*

248. Players] *Q1, Q3;* Playes *Q2.*
248.1. *Exeunt*] *Coxeter; Exit Q1; not
in Q2–3.*
250. S.D. EXIT] *Q1; not in Q2–3.*

---

241. *above . . . length*] referring to his name "Tallboy."
253. *purgation*] action of clearing themselves from suspicion of guilt.

Abuses Stripp'd and Whipp'd among 'em; with a-hey, Master Hearty, you are not merry:

Enter Sentwell.

and a-hey, Master Sentwell, where are your *Dramatis Personae*, your *Prologus*, and your *Actus Primus*, ha? Ha' they given you the slip for fear of the whip? A-hey.   260

SENTWELL.

A word aside, an't please you.

Sentwell takes Clack *aside, and gives him a paper.*

OLDRENTS.

I have not known a man in such a humor.

HEARTY.

And of his own finding! He stole it, indeed, out of his own bottles, rather than be robb'd of his liquor. Misers use to tipple themselves so.   265

OLDRENTS.

He does so outdo us, that we look like staid men again, Hearty, fine sober things.

HEARTY.

But how long will it last? He'll hang himself tomorrow for the cost we have put him to.

OLDRENTS.

I love a miser's feast dearly. To see how thin and scattering   270 the dishes stood, as if they fear'd quarreling.

HEARTY.

And how the bottles, to 'scape breaking one another, were brought up by one at once!

OLDRENTS.

How one of the serving-men, untrain'd to wait, spilt the white broth.   275

HEARTY.

And another, stumbling at the threshold, tumbled in his dish of rouncivals before him.

273. at once] *Q1;* and once! *Q2;*
and one! *Q3.*

---

256. *Abuses . . . Whipp'd*] a popular satire by George Withers (edn. 1613).
273. *by . . . once*] one at a time.
277. *rouncivals*] "a sort of great Peas, well known, and took name from Ronceval, a place at the foot of the Pyrenean Mountains, from whence they first came to us" (so Blount, *Glossography,* edn. 1674, quoted in *OED*).

OLDRENTS.

And most suitable to the niggardliness of his feast, we shall
now have an entertainment, or play, presented by beggars.

CLACK.

Send 'em in, Master Sentwell.   *Exit* Sentwell. 280
Sit, gentlemen; the players are ready to enter. And here's
a bill of their plays. You may take your choice.

OLDRENTS.

Are they ready for them all in the same clothes? Read 'em,
good Hearty.

HEARTY.

First, here's *The Two Lost Daughters*.   285

OLDRENTS.

Put me not in mind of the two lost daughters, I prithee.
What's the next?

HEARTY.

The Vagrant Steward.

OLDRENTS.

Nor of a vagrant steward. Sure some abuse is meant me.

HEARTY.

The Old Squire and the Fortune-teller.   290

OLDRENTS.

That comes nearer me. Away with it.

HEARTY.

The Beggar's Prophecy.

OLDRENTS.

All these titles may serve to one play, of a story that I
know too well. I'll see none of them.

HEARTY.

Then here's *The Merry Beggars*.   295

OLDRENTS.

Ay, that; and let 'em begin.

Enter Tallboy *and* Oliver.

TALLBOY.

The players are coming in; and Mistress Amie and your
man Martin are to be actors among 'em.

CLACK.

A-hey then for that, too. Some merry device, sure.

A flourish of shalms.

Hark! the beggars' hautboys. Now they begin.   300

OLDRENTS.

See, a most solemn Prologue.

Enter Poet *for Prologue.*

POET.

To knight, to squire, and to the gentles here,
We wish our play may with content appear.
We promise you no dainty wit of court,
Nor city pageantry, nor country sport: 305
But a plain piece of action, short and sweet;
In story true. You'll know it when you see't.

OLDRENTS.

True stories and true jests do seldom thrive on stages.

CLACK.

They are best to please you with this though, or a-hey with
a whip for them tomorrow.   310

OLDRENTS.

Nay, rather than they shall suffer, I will be pleas'd,
let 'em play their worst.

A flourish. Enter Patrico, *with* Lawyer *habited like* Oldrents.

See our patrico among 'em.

HEARTY.

That offered you a doxy in the barn.

PATRICO.

Your children's fortunes I have told,   315
That they shall beg ere they be old.
And will you have a reason why?
'Tis justice in their destiny.—

302. gentles] *this edition;* gentles   312.1. *with* Lawyer] *Q1; with a*
Q1–2; genteels *Q3.*   Lawyer *Q2–3.*
309. They are] *Q1–2;* they'd *Q3.*

299.1. *shalms*] or "shawms," a medieval musical instrument of the oboe
class having a double reed enclosed in a globular mouthpiece. (See John
H. Long, *Shakespeare's Use of Music* [Gainesville: Univ. of Florida Press,
1955], pp. 20–21.)

300. hautboys] "A wooden double-reed wind instrument of high pitch,
having a compass of about $2\frac{1}{2}$ octaves, forming a treble to the bassoon"
(*OED*).

CLACK.

Justice, ha! Are you meddling with justices already?

PATRICO.

>*Your grandfather, by crafty wile*   320
Of bargaining did much beguile
A thriftless heir of half the lands
That are descended to your hands.
And then by law, not equity,
Forc'd him and his posterity   325
To woe and shameful beggary.

LAWYER.

That was no fault of mine, nor of my children.

PATRICO.

>*But our forefathers' debts and crimes,*
Although forborne till future times,
Are not so paid. But what needs more,   330
I wish you happy in your store.   *Exit.*

OLDRENTS.

Dost note this, Hearty?

HEARTY.

You said you would be pleas'd, let 'em play their worst.

Lawyer *walks sadly, beats his breast, &c. To him enter* Soldier, *like*
Hearty, *and seems to comfort him.*

OLDRENTS [*aside*].

It begins my story, and by the same fortune-teller that
told me my daughters' fortunes, almost in the same words. 335
I know him now. And he speaks in the play to one that
personates me, as near as they can set him forth.

CLACK.

How like you it, sir? You seem displeas'd. Shall they be
whipp'd yet? A-hey, if you say the word.

OLDRENTS.

Oh, by no means, sir; I am pleas'd.   340

SOLDIER.

>*Sad for the words of a base fortune-teller?*
Believe him! Hang him. I'll trust none of 'em.

---

329. *forborne*] not urged or exacted.

They have all whims and double double meanings
In all they say.

OLDRENTS.

Whom does he talk or look like now?   345

HEARTY.

It is no matter whom. You are pleas'd, you say.

SOLDIER.

Ha' you no sack i'th'house? Am not I here?
And never without a merry old song?

            Sing.

Old sack, and old songs, and a merry old crew,
Will fright away cares when the ground looks blue.—   350
And can you think on gypsie fortune-tellers?

LAWYER.

I'll think as little of 'em as I can.

SOLDIER.

Will you abroad then? But here comes your steward.

            Enter Springlove *to* Lawyer.

OLDRENTS.

Bless me! Is not that Springlove?

HEARTY.

Is that you that talks to him, or that cockscomb I, do   355
you think? Pray let 'em play their play: the justice will
not hinder 'em, you see; he's asleep.

SPRINGLOVE.

Here are the keys of all my charge, sir. And
My humble suit is that you will be pleas'd
To let me walk upon my known occasions this summer.   360

LAWYER.

Fie! Canst not yet leave off those vagancies?
But I will strive no more to alter nature.
I will not hinder thee, nor bid thee go.

347. not I] *Q1–2;* I not *Q3.*   361. vagancies] *Q1–2;* Vagrancies
                                              Q3.

349–350.] See IV.i.224–227, note.

355. *cockscomb*] contemptuous expression for a young fellow.

361. *vagancies*] "A wandering or strolling" (a rare word listed only for
Brome in *OED*).

OLDRENTS.

My own very words at his departure.

HEARTY.

No matter. Pray attend.   365

LAWYER.

Come, friend. I'll take your counsel.   Exeunt Lawyer [*and*] Soldier.

SPRINGLOVE.

I've striven with myself to alter nature in me
For my good master's sake, but all in vain;
For beggars, cuckoo-like, fly out again
In their own notes and season.   370

Enter Rachel, Meriel, Vincent, Hilliard.

RACHEL.

Our father's sadness will not suffer us
To live in's house.

MERIEL.   *And we must have a progress.*

VINCENT.

Th'assurance of your loves hath engag'd us—

HILLIARD.

To wait on you in any course.

RACHEL.

Suppose we'll go a-begging.

VINCENT, HILLIARD.   *We are for you.*   375

SPRINGLOVE.

And that must be your course, and suddenly,
To cure your father's sadness: who is told
It is your destiny, which you may quit
By making it a trick of youth and wit.
I'll set you in the way.

ALL 4.   *But how? But how?*   380

All talk aside.

OLDRENTS.

My daughters and their sweethearts, too. I see
The scope of their design, and the whole drift
Of all their action now with joy and comfort.

---

369. *cuckoo-like*] seasonally, like the cuckoo; cf. Denham's *A Collection of Proverbs and Popular Sayings* in *Percy Society*, XX (1846): "The cuckoo comes of mid march, and cucks of mid Aperill; and gauns away of Midsummer month, When the corn begins to fill."

HEARTY.

But take no notice yet. See a whim more of it. But the
mad rogue that acted me, I must make drunk anon.   385

SPRINGLOVE.

Now! Are you all resolv'd?

ALL 4.   *Agreed, agreed.*

SPRINGLOVE.

You beg to absolve your fortune, not for need.   *Exeunt.*

OLDRENTS.

I must commend their act in that. Pray thee, let's call
'em and end the matter here. The purpose of their play
is but to work my friendship, or their peace with me; and 390
they have it.

HEARTY.

But see a little more, sir.

Enter Randall.

OLDRENTS.

My man Randall, too! Has he a part with 'em?

RANDALL.

They were well set a work, when they made me a player.
What is that I must say? And how must I act now? Oh! 395
That I must be steward for the beggars in Master Steward's
absence, and tell my master he's gone to measure land for
him to purchase.

OLDRENTS.

You, sir. Leave the work you can do no better (I can
forbear no longer) and call the actors back again to 400
me.

RANDALL.

With all my heart. And glad my part is so soon done.   *Exit.*

Enter Patrico.

PATRICO.

Since you will then break off our play,
Something in earnest I must say;
But let affected rhyming go.   405
I'll be no more a patrico.
My name is Wrought-on. Start not. But (if you

Desire to hear what's worth your best attention,
More privately) you may draw nearer me.

Oldrents *goes to him.*

HEARTY.
  Hear no more fortunes.
OLDRENTS.   You shall give me leave.   410
PATRICO.
  I am grandson to that unhappy Wrought-on,
Whom your grandfather craftily wrought out
Of his estate. By which, all his posterity
Were, since, expos'd to beggary. I do not charge
You with the least offense in this. But now   415
Come nearer me, for I must whisper to you.

Patrico *takes* Oldrents *aside.*

  I had a sister, who among the race
Of beggars was the fairest. Fair she was
In gentle blood, and gesture to her beauty,
Which could not be so clouded with base clothing   420
But she attracted love from worthy persons,
Which (for her meanness) they express'd in pity,
For the most part. But some assaulted her
With amorous, though loose desires, which she
Had virtue to withstand. Only one gentleman   425
(Whether it were by her affection, or
His fate to send his blood a-begging with her,
I question not) by her, in heat of youth,
Did get a son, who now must call you father.
OLDRENTS.
  Me?
PATRICO.   You. Attend me, sir. Your bounty then   430
Dispos'd your purse to her, in which, besides
Much money (I conceive by your neglect)
Was thrown this holy relic. Do you know it?

---

419. *gesture*] grace of manner.
419. *to*] in addition to.
431. *Dispos'd*] bestowed.

OLDRENTS.

The *Agnus Dei* that my mother gave me
Upon her deathbed! Oh, the loss of it   435
Was my sore grief; and now with joy it is
Restor'd by miracle! Does your sister live?

PATRICO.

No, sir. She died within a few days after
Her son was born, and left him to my care;
On whom I, to this day, have had an eye   440
In all his wanderings.

OLDRENTS.   Then the young man lives!

Enter Springlove, Vincent, Hilliard, Rachel, Meriel.

PATRICO.

Here with the rest of your fair children, sir.

OLDRENTS.

My joy begins to be too great within me!
My blessing, and a welcome to you all.
Be one another's, and you all are mine.   445

VINCENT, HILLIARD.

We are agreed on that.

RACHEL.   Long since.

We only stood till you shook off your sadness.

MERIEL.

For which we were fain to go a-begging, sir.

OLDRENTS.

Now I can read the justice of my fate,
And yours—

CLACK.   Ha! Justice? Are they handling of justice?   450

OLDRENTS.

But more applaud great providence in both.

CLACK.

Are they jerring of justices? I watch'd for that.

HEARTY.

Ay, so methought. No, sir. The play is done.

Enter Sentwell, Amie, Oliver, Martin.

---

434. *Agnus Dei*] a metal on which is stamped a figure of a lamb bearing
a cross or flag, as an emblem of Christ.

SENTWELL.

See, sir, your niece presented to you.

Springlove *takes* Amie.

CLACK.

What, with a speech by one of the players?   455
Speak, sir, and be not daunted. I am favorable.

SPRINGLOVE.

Then, by your favor, sir, this maiden is my wife.

CLACK.

Sure you are out o' your part. That is to say,
You must begin again.

SPRINGLOVE.

She's mine by solemn contract, sir.   460

CLACK [*to* Amie].

You will not tell me that. Are not you my niece?

AMIE.

I dare not, sir, deny't; we are contracted.

CLACK.

Nay, if we both speak together, how shall we hear one
another!

MARTIN.

I must disprove the contract.   465

TALLBOY.

That is my part to speak.

SENTWELL.

None can disprove it. I am witness to it.

CLACK.

Nay, if we all speak—as I said before.

OLDRENTS.

Hear me for all then. Here are no beggars (you are but
one, Patrico), no rogues, nor players: but a select company, 470
to fill this house with mirth. These are my daughters;
these their husbands; and this that shall marry your niece,
a gentleman, my son. I will instantly estate him in a
thousand pound a year to entertain his wife, and to their
heirs forever. Do you hear me now?   475

CLACK.

Now I do hear you. And I must hear you. That is to say,
it is a match. That is to say—as I said before.

TALLBOY.

And must I hear it, too? Oh—

OLDRENTS.

Yes, though you whine your eyes out.

HEARTY.

Nephew Martin, still the child with a suck-bottle of sack.   480
Peace, lamb, and I'll find a wife for thee.

OLDRENTS.

Now, patrico, if you can quit your function,
To live a moderate gentleman, I'll give you
A competent annuity for your life.

PATRICO.

I'll be, withal, your faithful beadsman, and spend my   485
whole life in prayers for you and yours.

CLACK.

And now, Clerk Martin, give all the beggars my free pass,
without all manner of correction! That is to say, with
a-hey, get 'em gone.

OLIVER.

Are not you the gentleman that challeng'd me in right of   490
your friend here?

VINCENT.

Your inspection's good, sir.

RACHEL.

And you the gentleman (I take it) that would have made
beggar-sport with us, two at once.

MERIEL.

For twelvepence apiece, sir.   495

OLIVER.

I hope we all are friends.

SPRINGLOVE.

Now, on my duty, sir, I'll beg no more
But your continual love and daily blessing.

OLDRENTS.

Except it be at court, boy, where if ever I come, it shall
be to beg the next fool-royal's place that falls.   500

---

482. *function*] present activity or trade.

487. *free pass*] an order by which vagrants or indigent persons are sent
to their place of abode.

499. *at court*] an allusion to Brome's *The Court Beggar*, acted at the Cockpit
c. 1639–1640.

SPRINGLOVE.

A begging Epilogue yet would not be,
Methinks, improper to this comedy.

Epilogue.

Tho' we are, now, no beggars of the crew,
We count it not a shame to beg of you.
The justice, here, has given his pass free   505
To all the rest unpunish'd; only we
Are under censure, till we do obtain
Your suffrages, that we may beg again;
And often, in the course we took today,
Which was intended for your mirth, a play;   510
Not without action, and a little wit.
Therefore we beg your pass for us and it.

FINIS

Appendix

Chronology

Approximate years are indicated by *.

Political and Literary Events	*Life and Major Works of Brome*

1558
Accession of Queen Elizabeth I.
Robert Green born.
Thomas Kyd born.

1560
George Chapman born.

1561
Francis Bacon born.

1564
Shakespeare born.
Christopher Marlowe born.

1572
Thomas Dekker born.*
John Donne born.
Massacre of St. Bartholomew's Day.

1573
Ben Jonson born.*

1574
Thomas Heywood born.*

1576
The Theatre, the first permanent public theater in London, established by James Burbage.
John Marston born.

1577
The Curtain theater opened.
Holinshed's *Chronicles of England, Scoland and Ireland.*

Drake begins circumnavigation of
the earth; completed 1580.
1578
John Lyly's *Euphues: The Anatomy
of Wit.*
1579
John Fletcher born.
Sir Thomas North's translation of
Plutarch's *Lives.*
1580
Thomas Middleton born.
1583
Philip Massinger born.
1584
Francis Beaumont born.*
1586
Death of Sir Philip Sidney.
John Ford born.
Kyd's *THE SPANISH TRAGEDY.*
1587
The Rose theater opened by
Henslowe.
Marlowe's *TAMBURLAINE,* Part
I.*
Execution of Mary, Queen of Scots.
Drake raids Cadiz.
1588
Defeat of the Spanish Armada.
Marlowe's *TAMBURLAINE,* Part
II.*
1589
Greene's *FRIAR BACON AND
FRIAR BUNGAY.*
Marlowe's *THE JEW OF
MALTA.*
1590
Spenser's *Faerie Queene* (Books I–III)   Birth.*
published.
Sidney's *Arcadia* published.
Shakespeare's *HENRY VI,* Parts
I–III,* *TITUS ANDRONICUS.*
1591
Shakespeare's *RICHARD III.*

1592

Marlowe's *DOCTOR FAUSTUS** and *EDWARD II.**

Shakespeare's *TAMING OF THE SHREW** and *THE COMEDY OF ERRORS.**

Death of Greene.

1593

Shakespeare's *LOVE'S LABOR'S LOST;* Venus and Adonis* published.

Death of Marlowe.

Theaters closed on acount of plague.

1594

Shakespeare's *TWO GENTLE-MEN OF VERONA;* The Rape of Lucrece* published.

Shakespeare's company becomes Lord Chamberlain's Men.

Death of Kyd.

1595

The Swan theater built.

Sidney's *Defense of Poesy* published.

Shakespeare's *ROMEO AND JULIET,* A MIDSUMMER NIGHT'S DREAM,* RICHARD II.**

Raleigh's first expedition to Guiana.

1596

Spenser's *Faerie Queene* (Books IV–VI) published.

Shakespeare's *MERCHANT OF VENICE,* KING JOHN.**

James Shirley born.

1597

Bacon's *Essays* (first edition).

Shakespeare's *HENRY IV*, Part I.*

1598

Demolition of The Theatre.

Shakespeare's *MUCH ADO ABOUT NOTHING,* HENRY IV, Part II.**

Jonson's *EVERY MAN IN HIS HUMOR* (first version).
Seven books of Chapman's translation of Homer's *Iliad* published.

1599
The Paul's Boys reopen their theater.
The Globe theater opened.
Shakespeare's *AS YOU LIKE IT*,* *HENRY V, JULIUS CAESAR*.*
Marston's *ANTONIO AND MELLIDA*,* Parts I and II.
Dekker's *THE SHOEMAKERS' HOLIDAY*.*
Death of Spenser.

1600
Shakespeare's *TWELFTH NIGHT*.*
The Fortune theater built by Alleyn.
The Children of the Chapel begin to play at the Blackfriars.

1601
Shakespeare's *HAMLET*,* *MERRY WIVES OF WINDSOR*.*
Insurrection and execution of the Earl of Essex.
Jonson's *POETASTER*.

1602
Shakespeare's *TROILUS AND CRESSIDA*.*

1603
Death of Queen Elizabeth I; accession of James VI of Scotland as James I.
Florio's translation of Montaigne's *Essays* published.
Shakespeare's *ALL'S WELL THAT ENDS WELL*.*
Heywood's *A WOMAN KILLED WITH KINDNESS*.
Marston's *THE MALCONTENT*.*
Shakespeare's company becomes the King's Men.

1604

Shakespeare's *MEASURE FOR MEASURE,* *OTHELLO.**

Marston's *THE FAWN.**

Chapman's *BUSSY D'AMBOIS.**

1605

Shakespeare's *KING LEAR.**

Marston's *THE DUTCH COURTE-SAN.**

Bacon's *Advancement of Learning* published.

The Gunpowder Plot.

1606

Shakespeare's *MACBETH.**

Jonson's *VOLPONE.**

Tourneur's *REVENGER'S TRAGEDY.**

The Red Bull theater built.

Death of John Lyly.

1607

Shakespeare's *ANTONY AND CLEOPATRA.**

Beaumont's *KNIGHT OF THE BURNING PESTLE.**

Settlement of Jamestown, Virginia.

1608

Shakespeare's *CORIOLANUS,* *TIMON OF ATHENS,* *PERICLES.**

Chapman's *CONSPIRACY AND TRAGEDY OF CHARLES, DUKE OF BYRON.**

Dekker's *Gull's Hornbook* published.

Richard Burbage leases Blackfriars theater for King's company.

John Milton born.

1609

Shakespeare's *CYMBELINE;**
Sonnets published.

Jonson's *EPICOENE.*

1610

Jonson's *ALCHEMIST.*

Chapman's *REVENGE OF BUSSY D'AMBOIS.**
Richard Crashaw born.

1611
Authorized (King James) Version of
the Bible published.
Shakespeare's *THE WINTER'S
TALE,* THE TEMPEST.**
Beaumont and Fletcher's *A KING
AND NO KING.*
Middleton's *A CHASTE MAID IN
CHEAPSIDE.**
Tourneur's *ATHEIST'S TRAG-
EDY.**
Chapman's translation of *Iliad* com-
pleted.

1612
Webster's *THE WHITE DEVIL.**

1613
The Globe theater burned.
Shakespeare's *HENRY VIII* (with
Fletcher).
Webster's *THE DUCHESS OF
MALFI.**
Sir Thomas Overbury murdered.

1614
The Globe theater rebuilt.   In service of Jonson as servant.
The Hope theater built.
Jonson's *BARTHOLOMEW FAIR.*

1616
Publication of Folio edition of
Jonson's *Works.*
Chapman's *Whole Works of Homer.*
Death of Shakespeare.
Death of Beaumont.

1618
Outbreak of Thirty Years War.
Execution of Raleigh.

1620
Settlement of Plymouth, Massa-
chusetts.

1621
Middleton's *WOMEN BEWARE WOMEN.* *
Robert Burton's *Anatomy of Melancholy* published.
Andrew Marvell born.

1622
Middleton and Rowley's *THE CHANGELING.* *
Henry Vaughan born.

1623
Publication of Folio edition of Shakespeare's *COMEDIES, HISTORIES, AND TRAGEDIES.*

Collaborates with Jonson in *A FAULT IN FRIENDSHIP* (lost).

1625
Death of King James I; accession of Charles I.
Death of Fletcher.

1626
Death of Tourneur.
Death of Bacon.

1627
Death of Middleton.

1628
Ford's *THE LOVER'S MELANCHOLY.*
Petition of Right.
Buckingham assassinated.

Listed among Queen of Bohemia's players in a warrant dated June 30.

1629

THE CITY WIT; * *THE LOVE-SICK MAID* (lost); *THE NORTHERN LASS.*

1631
Shirley's *THE TRAITOR.*
Death of Donne.
John Dryden born.

Answers a petition of complaint by John Bonus on same day it was filed, December 12.

1632
Massinger's *THE CITY MADAM.* *

THE NOVELLA; * *THE NORTHERN LASS* published; *THE QUEEN'S EXCHANGE.* *

1633
Donne's *Poems* published.
Death of George Herbert.

1634
Death of Chapman, Marston, Webster.*
Publication of *THE TWO NOBLE KINSMEN*, with title-page attribution to Shakespeare and Fletcher.
Milton's *Comus*.

Writing regularly (but not exclusively) for Company of Red Bull Players.
CHRISTIANETTA with George Chapman (lost);* *THE LIFE AND DEATH OF SIR MARTIN SKINK* with Thomas Heywood (lost);* *THE LATE LANCASHIRE WITCHES* with Thomas Heywood; *THE APPRENTICE PRIZE* with Thomas Heywood (lost).*

1635
Sir Thomas Browne's *Religio Medici*.

THE SPARAGUS GARDEN.
Signs a contract on July 20 with Salisbury Court Company giving them exclusive right to his plays.
THE NEW ACADEMY.

1636

*THE QUEEN AND CONCUBINE.**
Salisbury Court contract, according to Brome, canceled in May.
Seeks aid from William Beeston in August.
Composes *THE ANTIPODES* for William Beeston.*
Returns to Salisbury Court Company in October.
*THE JEWISH GENTLEMAN** (lost); *WIT IN MADNESS** (lost).

1637
Death of Jonson.

Commendatory verses for Thomas Nabbes's *MICROCOSMOS*.
Commendatory verses for Thomas Jordan's *Poetical Varieties*.
Commendatory verses for Shakerly Marmion's *Cupid and Psyche*.
THE ENGLISH MOOR.

1638

*THE DAMOISELLE;** *THE ANTIPODES* acted.

New contract with Salisbury Court Company in August to continue writing for another seven years but contract is not signed.

1639

First Bishops' War.
Death of Carew.*

Joins William Beeston at Cockpit Theater in May.
A MAD COUPLE WELL MATCH-ED.
Edits Fletcher's *MONSIEUR THOMAS* for publication.

1640

Short Parliament.
Long Parliament impeaches Laud.
Death of Massinger, Burton.

Lawsuit with Salisbury Court. Bill of Complaint on February 12 answered by Brome on March 6.
THE COURT BEGGAR; *THE ANTIPODES* published; *THE SPARAGUS GARDEN* published.
Verses in John Tatham's *The Fancy's Theater*.
Verses in Humphrey Mill's *A Night Search*.

1641

Irish rebel.
Death of Heywood.

A JOVIAL CREW.

1642

Charles I leaves London; Civil War breaks out.
Shirley's *COURT SECRET*.
All theaters closed by Act of Parliament.

1643

Parliament swears to the Solemn League and Covenant.

1645

Ordinance for New Model Army enacted.

1646

End of First Civil War.

1647

Army occupies London.
Charles I forms alliance with Scots.
Publication of Folio edition of

Commendatory verses in Folio edition of Beaumont and Fletcher's *COMEDIES AND TRAGEDIES*.

Beaumont and Fletcher's *COM-EDIES AND TRAGEDIES.*

1648
Second Civil War.

1649
Execution of Charles I.   Edits *Lacrymae Musarum.*

1650
Jeremy Collier born.

1651
Hobbes' *Leviathan* published.

1652
First Dutch War began (ended   *A JOVIAL CREW* published.
1654).
Thomas Otway born.

1653
Nathaniel Lee born.*   Mentioned as deceased.
                                          FIVE NEW PLAYS published.

1656
D'Avenant's *THE SIEGE OF RHODES* performed at Rutland House.

1657
John Dennis born.

1658
Death of Oliver Cromwell.
D'Avenant's *THE CRUELTY OF THE SPANIARDS IN PERU* performed at the Cockpit.

1659
                                          FIVE NEW PLAYS (second set)
                                          published.

1660
Restoration of Charles II.
Theatrical patents granted to Thomas Killigrew and Sir William D'Avenant, authorizing them to form, respectively, the King's and the Duke of York's Companies.

1661
Cowley's *THE CUTTER OF COLE-MAN STREET.*

D'Avenant's *THE SIEGE OF RHODES* (expanded to two parts).
1662
Charter granted to the Royal Society.
1663
Dryden's *THE WILD GALLANT.*
Tuke's *THE ADVENTURES OF FIVE HOURS.*
1664
Sir John Vanbrugh born.
Dryden's *THE RIVAL LADIES.*
Dryden and Howard's *THE IN-DIAN QUEEN.*
Etherege's *THE COMICAL RE-VENGE.*
1665
Second Dutch War began (ended 1667).
Great Plague.
Dryden's *THE INDIAN EMPEROR.*
Orrery's *MUSTAPHA.*
1666
Fire of London.
Death of James Shirley.

Oldrents, having "rescued" Springlove from vagrancy, cannot bear
for daughters to choose vagrancy —

Beggars → freedom